Hispano Homesteaders

The Last New Mexico Pioneers, 1850–1910

Peter –
We go back to
1969. and I'm proud of
the work we did
together

Harry

Hispano Homesteaders

The Last New Mexico Pioneers, 1850–1910

F. Harlan Flint

SUNSTONE
PRESS

SANTA FE

Sunstone books may be purchased for educational, business, or sales promotional use.
For information please write: Special Markets Department, Sunstone Press,
P.O. Box 2321, Santa Fe, New Mexico 87504-2321.

Book and Cover design › Vicki Ahl
Body typeface › Adobe Jenson Pro
Printed on acid-free paper

———————————————————————————————————————

Library of Congress Cataloging-in-Publication Data

Flint, F. Harlan, 1930-
  Hispano homesteaders : the last New Mexico pioneers, 1850-1910 / by F. Harlan Flint.
    p. cm.
  Includes bibliographical references.
  ISBN 978-0-86534-900-1 (softcover : alk. paper)
  1. Hispanic Americans--New Mexico--History--19th century. 2. Hispanic Americans--New
Mexico--History--20th century. 3. Pioneers--New Mexico--History--19th century. 4. Pioneers-
-New Mexico--History--20th century. 5. Frontier and pioneer life--New Mexico. 6. Community
life--New Mexico--History. 7. Mountain life--New Mexico--History. 8. New Mexico--
History--1848- 9. New Mexico--Social life and customs. 10. New Mexico--History, Local.
I. Title.
  F805.S75F55 2012
  305.868'0730789--dc23
                              2012028497

———————————————————————————————————————

WWW.SUNSTONEPRESS.COM
SUNSTONE PRESS / POST OFFICE BOX 2321 / SANTA FE, NM 87504-2321 /USA
(505) 988-4418 / ORDERS ONLY (800) 243-5644 / FAX (505) 988-1025

Hispano Homesteaders

The Last New Mexico Pioneers, 1850–1910

Contents

Preface

THE FINAL SURGE OF HISPANIC settlement into northern New Mexico and southern Colorado began close to the middle of the 1800s. It was about four decades later that a tiny settlement had its start at the far northern edge of New Mexico. That settlement will be a part of this story and can be seen as a microcosm of what was happening across the region in the culminating chapter of the centuries long expansion of what Richard L. Nostrand called "The Hispano Homeland."

Nostrand examined the unique New Mexico centered cultural community and its people, the Hispanos, and concluded that: "Because Hispanos adjusted to their natural environment, stamped it with their cultural impress, and created both from their natural environment and their cultural landscape a sense of place, their region is more than their locale—it is their homeland."

But who are these people? They have been called by many names: Hispanos, Hispanics, Latinos, Mexican Americans, Spanish Americans, Neomexicanos, Chicanos, Españoles Mexicanos and Nuevomexicanos. What we know is that their ancestors settled New Mexico in the early 1600s and had a very direct connection to Spain. Many among the first settlers came from the Iberian Peninsula or were only one generation removed from Spain. Some also shared the blood blend of Mexico.

These colonists had a strong sense of their Spanish identity and carried with them significant linguistic and cultural elements of their heritage. The concept of Spanish identity raises interesting questions. In the Middle Ages Spain was a diverse and conflicted place. In later centuries Spain came to be perhaps the most profoundly Catholic country in Europe but for about 800 years it was dominated by the Moors and Arabic was the cultural language of both Christians and Arabs in what was then called al-Andalus. Arabic was also spoken by the Jews who had been in the region since at least the third century. In medieval Spain they comprised the largest Jewish community in Western Europe.

During the long period of Moorish dominance, the Christians and Jews were relatively undisturbed in their religious practices but that tolerance ended as the reconquest was completed with the fall of Granada in 1492. In the same year King Ferdinand and Queen Isabella issued a royal decree ordering the expulsion from Spain of all Jews who refused to be converted to Christians. Those who converted and stayed came to be called conversos, marranos or new Christians. The same fate awaited the Islamist citizens of Spain who had known no other homeland for almost a millennium. In the next century many fled the country or at least nominally converted to Christianity. They were called moriscos. In the early 1600s, even those who converted were brutally ordered expelled.

The Muslim and Jewish ways of life had a profound effect on Spanish culture, language and traditions and despite Spanish efforts to extirpate all remnants of their historic presence, the two alien communities continued to be an irreversible part of the fabric of Spanish civilization and contributed to the gene pool of those who would settle the new world. The Jews continued to suffer at the hand of the Inquisition and many conversos went first to Mexico and later to New Mexico, attempting to distance themselves from the threat of Inquisition trials. Even sincerely believing conversos were at risk of being charged and convicted of heresy and suffering punishment that could be as extreme as being burned at the stake. Those who clung to their ancient beliefs were always at risk of being revealed.

Conversos were a part of New Mexico from its beginning. Many were among the original settlers. Recent research seems to prove that even Juan de Oñate, the first Spanish governor, had converso ancestors. Noted New Mexico historian Fray Angélico Chavez proudly claimed two conversos ancestors, one from Mexico and one from Portugal. Historian Stanley M. Hordes has spent decades studying what he calls New Mexico crypto Jews and has proven links between many twenty first century Hispano families with fifteenth century conversos.

So we see that the Spanish heritage that contributed to the genetic, ethnic and cultural make up of the New Mexico Hispano people was more complex and interesting than might have been expected. And in the years to come they lived and grew their communities in almost complete isolation from outside influence and with only very limited inflow of later immigrants from Mexico.

Because of their isolation from European influence, they continued to speak an archaic form of Spanish that drew heavily from their Castilian and Andalusian roots, sprinkled with a few words adopted from their new neighbors, the Pueblo Indians, and picked up from the Indian languages of Mexico. This rich legacy is recorded and celebrated in a book by Ruben Cobos, *A Dictionary of New Mexico and Southern Colorado Spanish*. Cobos identified many words and phrases used by these new world Hispanos that derived from the Spanish provinces from which the early settlers were drawn.

Another scholar of New Mexico Spanish did research in northern New Mexico and southern Colorado in the early years of the twentieth century. Aurelio M. Espinosa found that even in those recent years, Hispanos were speaking a version of castellano, the language of Cervantes. Equally important as the language is the persistence of songs, poems and folklore that originated in sixteenth and seventeenth century Spain and were still a part of New Mexico oral tradition in the twentieth century. Hundreds of long narrative poems and folk tales collected by Espinosa in the northern Hispano homeland remained virtually unchanged from their sixteenth century beginnings. Many other aspects of their Spanish traditions and patterns of life were also preserved.

The people drew on their historic experience to develop their distinctive New Mexico traditions. Formal education was limited in colonial New Mexico but strong oral traditions contributed to a wide variety of arts and crafts through which they expressed their religious faith and their artistic impulse. The Church and the Penitente brotherhood were incubators for many of the traditional crafts that produced the distinctive santos, retablos, alter screens, bultos and other media. Contemporary artists in these genres and others, such as tinwork, ironwork, straw appliqué, weaving and furniture making, continue to build on the ancient Spanish Colonial traditions.

The creation of the Hispano homeland began with the arrival of Juan de Oñate, who started the long, slow process of settlement and community building. The provincial capital of Santa Fe was established in about 1610. Over the next two centuries, interrupted by the Pueblo Revolt of 1680, the Spanish colonists slowly followed the rivers north, establishing small villages along the Rio Grande and its tributaries. Access to water dictated the path of development and continued to do so even into the early twentieth century.

Our main focus here will be the last stages of that historical process with the establishment of the first permanent villages in what is now southern Colorado and far northern New Mexico. As an example, we will look at the history of the communities of Los Pinos and San Miguel and more particularly a small dispersed community along five miles of the Rio de Los Pinos, known to the locals as Santa Rita. The little villages and dispersed settlements in the north were part of the last chapter in the history of Hispano settlement and expansion of the Hispano homeland. The people followed the little snow fed mountain streams north. These rivers were the foundation of their livelihood and their vigorous way of life.

The cultural strength of this unique community is surely attributable in large part to its physical isolation from the surge of immigration from Anglo-America that started in the mid 1800s. Even at the beginning of the twenty first century, its vitality can be seen in the optimism, creative adaptability and survival wisdom of the people we know in Santa Rita Canyon and the other surviving communities of this region.

For years my family and I have been getting acquainted with the little New Mexico and Colorado villages and the people who live there now. In conversations with neighbors and other Valley residents we have learned that almost all people of Hispano heritage know where in New Mexico their parents or grandparents came from. Most of the pioneer settlers came from places like Abiquiu, Ojo Caliente, Española, El Rito, Taos or places that no longer exist.

When the people first came to the southern San Luis Valley all the little villages were in New Mexico. Now most of them are in Colorado. Because of accidents of history, the two New Mexico villages of San Miguel and Los Pinos find themselves across a state line from their old neighbors in Colorado.

I became interested in the history of the place over thirty years ago when my family acquired property on the Rio de Los Pinos that included a typical old jacal style farm house, probably built over a hundred years ago by the original Hispano owner of the homestead patent on the land. My curiosity about the place and its people who came here more than a century ago, made me want to learn more about these pioneers and what brought them to what was then the northern edge of their world.

—F. Harlan Flint

Santa Rita Canyon and the San Luis Valley

THE SETTLEMENT OF A RURAL COMMUNITY on the upper end of the Rio de Los Pinos will be discussed in greater detail later. We begin with a brief physical and geographic sketch of the place and its neighborhood. The map of Northern New Mexico and Southern California depicts the area of interest.

The local area became known as Santa Rita Canyon, given its name by the Hispano pioneers that settled there. It is a section of the Rio de Los Pinos valley beginning about three miles upstream from the village of San Miguel and extending about five miles west along the river to the Toltec Gorge. The elevation ranges from about 8400 feet to about 9000 feet at the entrance to the Toltec Gorge. The small inholdings of private land are surrounded by the Carson National Forest and the Cruces Basin Wilderness. The place is in New Mexico's Rio Arriba County, about 100 road miles from the county seat in Tierra Amarilla. To the north at a distance of about a mile is the Colorado state line and the county of Conejos,

Because of the northern latitude and the high elevation, the growing season is short and today, in the absence of any full time residents, the Canyon is usually inaccessible for much of the long, cold winters because of frequent heavy snows. It is not uncommon to record winter temperatures as low as minus 30 degrees Fahrenheit and the ice is usually not off the river until April.

The headwaters of the river are in a Colorado wilderness area a few miles west and north of the Toltec Gorge through which the water cascades down about a thousand feet from the high meadows up above. After passing through Santa Rita Canyon, the river flows east through the tiny New Mexico villages of San Miguel and Los Pinos and joins the Rio San Antonio near Antonito, Colorado. The merged rivers join the Conejos River which ultimately flows into the Rio Grande.

While the Santa Rita Canyon is in New Mexico, it is on the edge of Colorado's San Luis Valley and is culturally and geographically a part of that dramatic physical environment which has shaped the history and development of the Valley and the region. The high, semi-arid valley is in the rain shadow of the imposing mountain ranges that encircle it with peaks of 10,000 to over 14,000 feet.

To the east is the Sangre de Cristo range, the southern end of the Rocky Mountains, reaching all the way to Santa Fe. On the west is the rugged wilderness of the San Juan Range that forms a part of the continental divide. Guarding the southern entrance to the Valley is the imposing San Antonio Mountain. Between these lofty barriers lies the 7500 foot high valley extending about 120 miles north and south and 65 miles east and west. Because of the mountains, the valley receives only a few inches of precipitation each year. But the mountains that steal the valley's rain and snow give it back generously in runoff from the usually abundant winter snowfall that also recharges the valley's massive aquifers. All the streams flow from the surrounding mountains toward the center of the valley and the Rio Grande, which bisects the valley as it begins its 1800 mile journey to the Gulf of Mexico.

These many tributary streams of the Rio Grande were the life giving force for the Utes and other Indian tribes who lived there. They were also the magnet for the Hispano pioneers who came to the valley from the south and for the later wave of settlers from the east. The Rio de Los Pinos is one of the southernmost contributors to the hydrologic miracle of the San Luis Valley and provided early sites for permanent settlement.

Map of Northern New Mexico and Southern Colorado.

The Early Years

THE PERIOD OF SPANISH EXPLORATION in New Mexico began with the expedition of Francisco Coronado in 1540 and 1541. There followed a series of entradas and finally, in 1598, an expedition led by Juan de Oñate created the first settlement in the Rio Grande valley at San Gabriel, across the Rio Grande from what is now the Okay Owingeh Pueblo, formerly known as San Juan. In 1609 Pedro de Peralta was named Governor and Santa Fe became the capital of the province. From that time until the Pueblo Revolt of 1680, Santa Fe grew slowly and the Spanish began occupying land in the vicinity of various Pueblo villages under a system called encomiendas. The encomienda grants to soldiers and colonists gave them the privilege of using Indian land and labor, nominally in exchange for protection from marauding Indians and the added "benefit" of conversion to the Catholic faith, usually an unwelcome gift. The Spanish also granted lands known as estancias to colonists for farming and stock raising.

By the time of the Pueblo Revolt about 2500 colonists lived in New Mexico, but Santa Fe was the only official town or villa. The rest of the Spanish population, including the friars and their missions, were associated with communities of Pueblo Indians in the valley of the Rio Grande and some of its tributaries. The Revolt forced the colonist out of New Mexico and down the Rio Grande to the vicinity of what is now El Paso. Prior to that disaster their tenuous control of territory stretched roughly from Taos in the north to Socorro in the south. The area north of the still familiar La Bajada hill was called Rio Arriba and the area to the south was Rio Abajo.

Diego de Vargas began the reconquest of New Mexico in 1692 and recaptured Santa Fe in 1693, but it was not until close to the end of the century that the defeat of the Pueblos was complete and the Spanish could once again contemplate expansion to the north.

The Northern Push

S HORTLY AFTER THE REOCCUPATION of Santa Fe in 1693, new villas and settlements began to be established north of the capital. In 1695, a group of families from Santa Fe founded the villa of Santa Cruz, about twenty miles north of Santa Fe. In the next few years Hispanos from Santa Fe and Santa Cruz began to move into areas in the Rio Grande valley and along some of the tributary streams.

Under Spanish law the executive power of provincial government in New Mexico belonged to the governor. He was usually also the military leader and carried the dual title of gobernador y capitán general. The governor also was given the power to make land grants. After the reconquest the governor began making land grants, starting with grants to the Pueblos and to individuals being rewarded for their roles in the reconquest. But his main motivation was to encourage the expansion of settlement.

Land grants varied considerably but fell into two broad categories: private grants and community grants. Private grants were to individuals and their families and were usually fairly small. If perfected by occupation and use, they became the private property of the grantee and could be passed on to heirs or sold to others.

Community grants were made to large groups of families and were the principal vehicle for creating new plaza villages. Each family would receive a small tract for its own use as homestead and irrigated farm land. These tracts were called suertes. The remaining large acreage within the grant boundaries were called the ejido and were reserved to be used by all the grant holders. The ejido was the equivalent of the commons and was used for grazing, hunting, fire wood and timber harvesting. The common lands could not be sold and were to be preserved in perpetuity for community use.

The colonists were village people by custom and necessity. They banded close together for purposes of self defense and they collaborated to provide their communities with water for irrigation and domestic use. Water was an organizing principle in the northern expansion. The smaller tributary streams lent themselves to the creation of community irrigation ditches, acequias, and the settlers were mutually dependant in the construction and maintenance of these facilities. The upstream head gates were on the property of one settler and the ditch crossed the property of the many other people who were served as the water made its way down along the river. And as the families and villages grew the people were on the lookout for new streams and irrigable lands that could support new villages. These acequias, are a unique feature of New Mexico life and are treated under state law as quasi governmental entities. The Moors brought this institution with them when they occupied Spain in the middle ages.

We think of New Mexico as a dry, high desert and of course it is a very dry place. Most of the state receives less than ten inches of precipitation per year. But, in a strange way, New Mexico is a place of rivers. Because they are few and small, they seem even more consequential. The history of New Mexico is really the history of the Rio Grande basin. With few exceptions, settlement and the expansion of the Hispano Homeland was driven by the big river and its many small tributaries. In order to grow the community the people literally followed the rivers north. There were two paths of settlement. One followed the eastern Rio Grande tributary streams north to Taos and the other villages and finally on to Colorado. The other path pursued the western tributaries north to Abiquiu, Ojo Caliente and ultimately to Colorado. One route led to San Luis, the first European village in Colorado and the other to Guadalupe, later called Conejos on the western edge of the San Luis Valley. Our map of the Rio Grande and some of its tributaries roughly depicts the main stream of the Rio Grande and some of the small streams that permitted and supported the pattern of settlement.

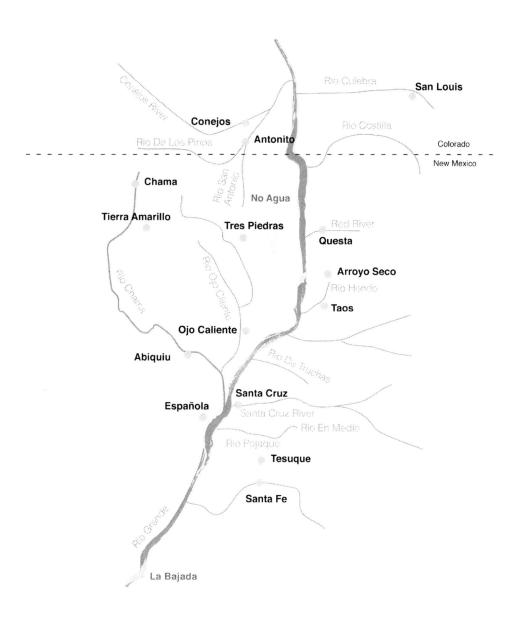

Map of the Rio Grande and some of its tributaries.

It would be impossible to show all the small streams given names by Hispano pioneers but here is a partial list of the principle eastern and western tributaries of the upper Rio Grande:

East Side:

    Santa Fe River
    Rio Tesuque
    Rio Chapulin
    Rio en Medio (Rio Molino)
    Poquaque Creek (Rio Chupadero)
    Rita Gallina
    Rito de Juan Manuel
    Rio Quemado
    Santa Cruz river
    Rio de Truchas (Rio de La Cebolla, Rio San Leonardo)
    Rio Nutrias
    Rio de Las Trampas
    Rio Lucio
    Rio Enbudo
    Rio Santa Barbara
    Rio Grande del Rancho
    Rio Pueblo de Taos
    Rio de La Olla
    Rio Chiquito
    Rio Fernando de Taos
    Rio Lucero
    Arroyo Seco
    Rio Hondo
    Red Riber (Rio Colorado)
    Columbine Creek
    San Cristobal Creek
    Latir Creek
    Cabresto Creek
    Costilla Creek

West Side

Rio Chama
Rio Ojo Caliente
El Rito Creek (Rita Colorado)
Rio de Las Tusas
Rio Vallecito
Rio de Los Pinos
Rio San Antonio
Rio Frijoles

Other Chama Tributaries:

Rio Gallina
Rio Brazos
Willow Creek
Rio Chamita
Boulder Creek
Wolf Creek
Rio Cebloa
Rio del Oso

Local people would be able to put names to dozens more little streams in their neighborhoods.

The map also suggests the vast areas of New Mexico that are unwatered and therefore inhospitable to human habitation. It also shows the often adventurous footsteps required to move from one small oasis to the next and then the next. Where there was no surface water there would be no settlement and where water was present, the people would come.

In early 1695, Diego de Vargas made the grant that would establish the first post revolt settlement north of Santa Fe. It was given the imposing title of "Villa Nueva de Santa Cruz del Rey Nuestro Señor Carlos II de Españoles Mexicanos." In the next two decades numerous additional grants led to the creation of many new plaza villages along the Rio Grande and its tributaries and to the west along the Rio Chama and its tributaries. On the Rio Grande, the new places would include Los Luceros (1712), Embudo (1725) and what is now Velarde in 1775. Then, roughly following the path of what is now known as "the high road to Taos," the Hispano farmers settled in Chimayo, Las Trampas (1751), Cordova, Truchas (1754) and Rodarte in the Penasco area. On the Chama and its tributaries, land grants led to the settlement of Puesta de Abiquiu which became known as Santa Rosa de Lima (1734), and Ojo Caliente which may have been settled as early as 1731. Other grants along El Rito Creek (Rito Colorado) led to several new places including what is now the village of El Rito.

We interrupt the narrative to examine in more detail what happened in Taos. Before the Pueblo Revolt of 1680, Spanish officials had long recognized the rich prospects for settlement in that well watered region. There were pre- revolt efforts to settle there and missionary priests had been assigned to the Pueblo, whose people adamantly resisted Spanish incursion and influence. In 1640, pueblo residents killed their priest and, expecting retribution, they abandoned the pueblo and fled to live with the Apaches in what is now western Kansas. After a twenty year absence they returned to their home and subsequently played a major role in the Pueblo Revolt that sent the Spanish south to Texas.

After the Revolt was quashed, settlers were eager to resume their efforts in the Taos area. There were early attempts to renew old grants and seek new ones but conflicts with the Pueblo over water and frequent raids by Commanches and other nomadic Indians made life difficult for both the pueblo and potential settlers. Official Spanish control was initiated with the appointment of an alcalde mayor in 1715. Spanish land grants began to be issued to the Hispanos who recognized the land and irrigation potential of the Taos basin. However the grantees had great difficulty completing their occupation, establishing residency and cultivating their land. One of the earliest of the post Revolt grants was for lands in the area of what is now Ranchos de Taos but it was probably not actually settled until 1724 or later. Progress was halting and tortuous. In 1750, a church census reported a Taos area non-pueblo Indian population of 136 people in twenty three families. Most of these people probably lived in Ranchos de Taos. The tenuous safety of both the Pueblo and the Hispanos was made clear by a Commanche raid in 1760 that killed seventeen people and resulted in the capture of fifty six women and children from the Hispano community. As a result, most of the survivors abandoned their farms and ranchos and moved into the Pueblo for their mutual protection. Over the course of the next two decades, the settlers cautiously returned to their farms and plazas. In 1796, the creation of the village of Taos was finally formalized with the issuance of the Don Fernando de Taos Grant.

In the same year, the Taos alcalde (mayor) conducted a census of the communities under his jurisdiction. It showed 510 people at Taos Pueblo, 196 at Picuris Pueblo and 779 Hispanos. The Hispanos were reported to be living in six "plazas":

Plaza de San Francisco (Ranchos de Taos)
Plaza de San Gertrudis
Plaza de Nuestra Señora de Guadalupe (village of Taos)
Plaza de la Purísima (Upper Ranchitos)
Plaza de San Francisco de Paula (Lower Ranchitos)
Plaza de Nuestra Señora de los Dolores (Cañon)

A definitive history of the land grants, settlement patterns and acequia construction in the Taos area is provided by a 1990 study prepared for the New Mexico State Engineer by John O. Baxter. Baxter's report entitled "Spanish Irrigation in the Taos Valley" provides a remarkably detailed picture of the process that involved dozens of Spanish and Mexican land grants and shows the pivotal role of acequia construction in the intense development of this relatively water rich region.

As mentioned, the Hispano settlers returned to the area shortly after the reconquest of New Mexico following the Pueblo Revolt of 1880. In the time between the early 1700s and the end of the Mexican era in 1846, Baxter reported that over 80 acequias were built in the Taos area.

These amazing engineering achievements involved six Rio Grande tributaries: Rio Hondo, Arroyo Seco, Rio Lucero, Rio Pueblo de Taos and Rio Grande del Pueblo, plus its tributary, Rio Chiquito as shown in the following map.

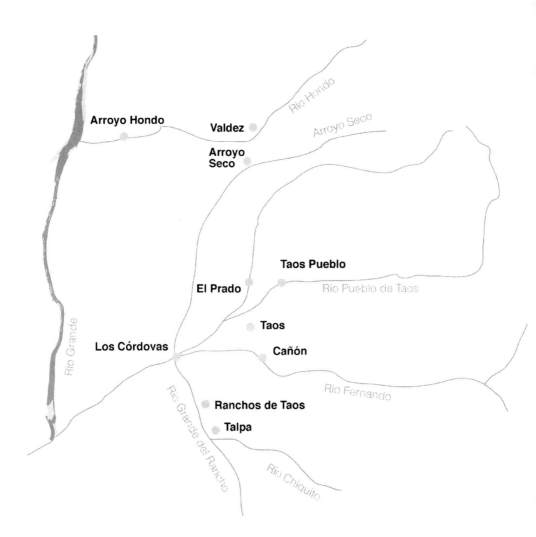

Map of Taos Area Tributaries

This history of acequia and community building in the Taos area dramatically demonstrates the centrality of the irrigation culture in the northern expansion of the Hispano homeland. The broader story is told in *Reining in the Rio Grande* by Fred W.Phillips, G. Emlen Hall and Mary E. Black. They tell us that between 1590 and 1846, four hundred acequias were built on upper Rio Grande tributaries and that those acequias irrigated as much as 55,000 acres.

Many of the Taos area acequias watered farms in narrow canyons between steep rocky cliffs that would have challenged the skills of even twenty first century engineers. The following quote from Baxter describes one project on the Rio Hondo in about 1815:

> In later years everyone agreed that building the Cuchilla acequia up the south wall of the Hondo Canyon was a remarkable feat, one that required all the ingenuity and manpower the settlers could master. Undaunted by lack of technical training and metal tools, New Mexico pioneers completed a major construction project, still regarded with awe by professional engineers. To locate the proper grade for carrying water to the top, someone devised a crude transit, triangular in shape with a sight made with a small piece of lead suspended by a thread from one corner. Workers also manufactured shovels and crow bars from fire hardened oak and other native wood to move large amounts of rocky soil.

Projects of this magnitude at that time and under those circumstances must have called upon all the help available from San Isidro, the Patron Saint of farmers and San Juan Nepomucino, the Patron Saint of irrigation. The Taos story is unique only in its scale. It would be repeated over and over in the other new places along the northern path.

Many of the other new villages had a precarious existence in the late eighteenth and early nineteenth centuries. The outlier villages, such as Abiquiu and Ojo Caliente were particularly vulnerable targets. The Utes and Comanches, sometimes as allies, frequently attacked the villages, as did the Navajos and Apaches. When this happened, people were often forced to retreat to Santa Cruz or Santa Fe. Even today, a visitor to the old adobe church in Ojo Caliente can see the gun ports high up in the walls of the church, used by the settlers to defend themselves.

Many of the people in these front line communities were genízaros, a term applied to a variety of people, often nomadic Indians with no clear tribal attachment and others of mixed Hispano and Indian blood, who came to or were sent to live in dangerous frontier areas of New Mexico, to settle there and provide a buffer against nomadic Indian raids. Genízaros often were Indian captives of inter tribal battles who were later sold into Spanish families in what can only be described as a form of slavery.

The Hispano people also participated in capturing and trading these unfortunate people, as did the Pueblos. It is perhaps a mitigating factor that the genízaros frequently came to be accepted as full members of the family and ultimately gained freedom and equality with their peers in the family. It is reported that many families did not distinguish between their full blood children and the genízaro members of the family when it came to important issues like inheritance.

The term genízaro was not an invention of these new world pioneers. It was a part of their ancestral memory. As early as the fifteenth century, Spain was the frequent victim of Ottoman pirate raids. These marauders were descendants of the Moors who were finally expelled from the Iberian Peninsula in the late 1400s after centuries of occupation. They returned to plunder their old homeland and also to take Christian hostages who were kept as slaves, sold, or sometimes compelled to serve as mercenary soldiers. The Ottoman Empire called its mercenary armies the Janissary Corps and they were known in Spanish as los genízaros. So, in both the old and new worlds, these people of mixed heritage became slaves and sometimes soldiers in other peoples' conflicts.

After almost another century of difficult challenges, the Hispano colony had managed to extend its reach, following the rivers north. Despite the many obstacles they had to overcome, their population in New Mexico had grown to about 16,000, perhaps double what it had been in 1680, and the people were poised to dramatically extend their reach in the next century.

The San Luis Valley Before Settlement

D
URING THE LONG PERIOD OF SPANISH exploration and settlement, the San Luis valley was the land of its native peoples. And it was a fiercely contested place even before the arrival of the Hispanos. In the north were the Cheyennes and Arapahoes. The Comanches were probably the most powerful of all the Indians in the early years and were dominant in the valley until late in the eighteenth century, The Navajos and Apaches also laid claim to the valley at times. The Utes claimed the San Luis valley as their ancestral homeland but they suffered mightily from the Comanches' military superiority for many decades. Partly as a result of one of the few Spanish military victories against the Comanches, the Utes finally prevailed and gained control of their mountains and plains in the San Luis valley.

Among the many things the Spanish brought to the new world, none would prove to be more consequential than the horse. There were no horses in the entire continent until the Spanish Conquistadors came to Mexico. The horse gave them an immense military advantage over the foot bound native people. It allowed the Spanish to move faster and farther than the Indians. It also had a devastating psychological impact on the natives who were awed and terrified by the imposing creatures. When Oñate came north to New Mexico in 1598 he arrived with seven hundred horses. Horses would change things forever for the native people.

The Spanish horses were the product of centuries of breeding and adaptation to the harsh, dry climate of southern Spain. They had originally come to the Iberian Peninsula from North Africa with the Moors who had invaded and occupied the peninsula for centuries. These horses were perfectly suited to Andalusia and Castile and therefore were a good fit for the dry mesa and canyon country of New Mexico and the semi-arid Great Plains to the east. They were small, fast and resilient. They could sustain themselves on the native grasses of the region, could survive even in the harsh, cold winters, and they could trail great distances without water. The horses served the Spanish well but would prove to be a perfect tool and weapon of the nomadic Indians of the west.

The more advanced village dwelling and agricultural people of the Pueblos had limited need for horses but the Apaches and other tribes soon recognized their value for travel, hunting and ultimately for war. By 1650, the Apaches were using horses to raid New Mexico villages and Pueblos. The Spanish tried to deprive Indians of horses, but it was a futile effort. Raiding Indians captured hundreds and ultimately thousands of horses and soon became skilled riders and horse breeders.

When the Pueblo Revolt drove the Spanish out of New Mexico, thousands of horses escaped and became the first generation of wild mustangs that thrived and reproduced in vast numbers. These free ranging animals and the horses captured in Indian raids became the stock that revolutionized the way Indians lived. They became accomplished riders and fearsome mounted warriors.

The story of the horse is an appropriate prelude to what was happening in the San Luis valley in the period before settlement and the central role played by the Utes. The Utes or Yutas as they were known in Spanish were a nomadic people although there is evidence that they often returned to the same camp sites year after year. Before the Spanish came and provided them with horses, they hunted and gathered and relied on human transport or perhaps dogs to move within their territory. The acquisition of horses by trade and war gave them the means to travel, hunt, trade and fight over a much larger area, and they became extremely accomplished horsemen.

The valley was rich in wildlife and the Utes lived well, hunting for deer, elk, antelope and mountain sheep as well as smaller animals and wildfowl. There were abundant buffalo in the valley during the early nineteenth century although the huge herds were on the plains to the east of the Sangre de Cristo Mountains. In the De Vargas Journal of 1694, the General reported on successful buffalo kills by his party.

The first recorded journey of exploration in the valley by the Spanish was the Diego de Vargas expedition of 1694, shortly after the recapture of New Mexico following the Pueblo Revolt. He traveled north from Taos, up the east side of the Rio Grande along the almost impenetrable gorge and forded the river near its junction with the Rio Culebra, not far from what is now San Luis, Colorado. Following a brief battle with the Utes which ended in a peaceful reconciliation, he spent a few days in the vicinity of what is now Antonito, Colorado.

On his way back south to Ojo Caliente and Santa Fe, he almost certainly crossed the Rio de Los Pinos, close to the site of the current villages of Ortiz, Colorado and Los Pinos, New Mexico. A reconstruction of his journey can be found in a book by Ruth Marie Colville, *La Vereda, A Trail through Time*, published by the San Luis Valley Historical Society in 1966.

While the de Vargas expedition was the first verified Spanish visit to the valley, there is evidence that the Utes had traveled to the south and traded with the settlers and Pueblos in New Mexico during much of the 1600s until the Pueblo revolt. They probably had more cordial relations with the Spanish than did the Pueblos, with good reason. The Pueblos lived under Spanish occupation and were often the victims of Ute and other Indian raids from which the Spanish authorities were unable to protect them.

By the middle of the eighteenth century the Utes often joined the Spanish in their confrontations with other nomadic tribes. It is likely that Hispano traders were frequent visitors to the San Luis Valley and the Utes went south to trade with the settlers. Later in the century the Utes joined the Spanish in an important military engagement against the Comanches who had been inflicting great damage on the settlers, the Pueblos and other Indian tribes for decades. Colville reported that in 1779, "... a large group, 'two hundred men of the Ute and Apache nation' joined Don Juan de Anza, Governor of New Mexico, ...at the Rio de Los Pinos."

They crossed the Rio Grande further north, circled south and inflicted a decisive defeat on the High Plains Comanches. The battle also resulted in the death of their notorious leader, Cuerno Verde (Green Horn), who had been punishing the colonists and the Pueblos for over a decade.

The de Anza victory is considered to have been one of the greatest triumphs ever achieved by the Spanish in their long running confrontation with the Comanches. He not only won the battle and killed Cuerno Verde, a much feared chief, but he also negotiated treaties with other Comanche chiefs that blunted Comanche warfare in New Mexico and laid the foundation for later settlement in the San Luis valley.

The long shadow of Spanish pressure from the south would soon challenge the hegemony of the Utes in their traditional homeland. The still distant pattern of western displacement of Indians to make way for American settlers was even more ominous but had not yet affected the Utes and other native people in the early part of the nineteenth century. By the 1830s the Americans were forcing the Indians in the southeastern states, even the "civilized tribes" like the Cherokees, to abandon their traditional homelands and move to the new congressionally designated "Indian Country" west of the Mississippi River. By the middle of the century the same fate would face the Utes and the other native people of the region.

On to the North

B Y THE BEGINNING OF THE NINETEENTH CENTURY, after almost two hundred years of Spanish sovereignty, the Hispano homeland still only stretched from Taos in the north to Sabinal in the south. However, the occupied area was much more densely populated with Hispanos than it had been a hundred years earlier. Because of persistent nomadic Indian raids, many people at the edges of the colony had retreated from the more dispersed ranchos and moved to fortified villages called plazas. Houses were built wall to wall with the neighboring properties and around a central plaza. The outside walls had no windows and the entrance to the plaza was a fortified gate. The settlers frequently built a torreón (tower) close by from which they could observe the approach of unfriendly visitors.

Despite the raids by Navajos, Apaches, Comanches and Utes, the pressure for expansion was strong. The de Anza expedition had contributed to a more peaceful period in the core territories. Traditional features of Hispano life were to change as the people moved north. Most of the settlers in the older plaza villages were farmers while those on the frontier were increasingly turning to stock raising, both sheep and cattle. The need for grazing land was a major motivation for extending the northern frontier.

Until about 1800, settlement had occurred through a process that Nostrand called "contiguous expansion." That is, a parent village would send off families to a nearby location and start a new village on a neighboring stream or further up on the same stream. In the new century, especially at its frontier edge, stockmen would move out to greater distances, find temporary pasture and perhaps start rudimentary irrigation and build rough structures for living, but return to the home village when winter came or Indians forced them to leave. These seasonal uses would provide the basis for later full time settlers to follow.

While our focus here is on the north, the process of contiguous expansion was also growing the area of settlement in the east, the west and the south. By the 1880s the Hispano homeland had expanded dramatically to places as distant as southern Arizona, west Texas and Oklahoma and the plains of eastern Colorado, as well as new locations in New Mexico.

Expansion to the north followed two paths, one on the east side of the Rio Grande and one on the west. On the east side, families from Taos moved north to create the village of Arroyo Hondo in 1815. Next came San Antonio (later called Valdez) and San Cristobal and then another San Antonio that was to become the present Questa. The last village below what would become the Colorado boundary was Costilla, founded in 1849.

On the west side of the Rio Grande, people from the lower Rio Chama valley were the source for northern settlement. Ojo Caliente and Abiquiu people created the plaza villages of Vallecito in 1824 and Petaca in 1836, plus additional ephemeral places that no longer exist. Vallecitos and Petaca were big step outs from where its settlers previously lived. The greater distance of these moves was necessary because of the lack of streams in the area capable of supporting settlers. In the area between Ojo Caliente to the Colorado border there are no live streams, except for the tiny Rio Tusas near Vallecitos and Petaca and the streams to the west of San Antonio Mountain. It is so dry there that the early pioneers called the region "No Agua" and some modern maps still retain that name.

The Americans Are Coming

THROUGHOUT THE LONG PERIOD from the first entrada until the Mexican Revolution of 1821, much of what is now Colorado, including the San Luis Valley, was claimed with some ambiguity by Spain and after the settlement of Santa Fe it was all part of the Province of New Mexico. This was true even though no Spaniard is documented to have set foot in the San Luis Valley until the late 1600s. When Mexico became independent, she asserted the same rights.

The United States, a relative late comer, acknowledged Spanish sovereignty in the region and after Mexican independence in 1821, the U.S. generally respected Mexican control, despite occasional conflict. The Mexican war of 1846–1848 imposed American sovereignty and the valley became part of the Territory of New Mexico.

The nineteenth century brought tumultuous change to the San Luis Valley, as it did to all of western America. For over two hundred years the growing threat of European incursion had been a noticeable but not revolutionary factor in the lives of the native inhabitants of the valley. Now what had been a distant threat was to become a tidal wave that by the end of the century would sweep away all but small remnants of the Ute Nation. And even as Spain and then Mexico were about to confirm their claims by settling the valley, they too would be gone before the middle of the century.

These dramatic and unanticipated changes were the result of political decisions and social dynamics taking place in a nation more than a thousand miles away. When the century began, the United States was a fairly small, twenty five year old country with a western boundary on the distant Mississippi River. When it ended, it was a young giant stretching from coast to coast and about to become a world power. With the Louisiana Purchase in 1803, the U.S. suddenly doubled its size and became the valley's next door neighbor with a western boundary along the Sangre de

Cristo Mountain range. This vast new territory was largely unexplored and unknown to Americans. The members of the Lewis and Clark Expedition in 1804 to 1806 were the first Americans to see much of the interior of western America.

The Spanish had been frequent visitors to the San Luis Valley for over a hundred years and the French had founded the city of New Orleans and had been nominal owners of the vast lands to the east, but the first American to see the valley probably came in about 1804.

In 1807, Lieutenant Zebulon Pike, commander of a United States Army expedition, erroneously or at least prematurely, planted the American flag on the bank of the Conejos River. He was promptly captured and expelled by the Spanish authorities, but he was a clear sign of things to come. A growing number of French Canadian trappers and American mountain men began to spend time in the area and traveled south to Taos and Santa Fe. The Spanish were generally hostile to the foreigners but with independence, the Mexican government in Santa Fe was much more tolerant and open to trade with the Americans. However, the Governor was properly concerned with the growing threat to Mexican sovereignty in the north as more easterners appeared on his frontier.

In an effort to encourage settlement in the twilight days of the brief Mexican era, the Governor made land grants in the southern part of the valley to New Mexico citizens. Ironically, those grants were not to be successfully pursued by the grantees until after Mexican control was extinguished by the Mexican War. There was no shooting war in New Mexico. In August of 1846, General S.W. Kearney marched unimpeded into Santa Fe and claimed New Mexico for the United States. The Treaty of Guadalupe Hidalgo in 1848 ended the two hundred and fifty year period of Spanish and Mexican rule. It resulted in adding to the United States the huge territory comprising most of the current states of California, Nevada, Utah, Arizona, New Mexico and Colorado, including the San Luis Valley.

It was during the decade of the 1840s and particularly during the one term presidency of James K. Polk that the American pursuit of manifest destiny was most rampant. President Polk was inaugurated in March, 1845 and it fell to him to implement the annexation treaty that President John Tyler had negotiated to acquire the Republic of Texas. Mexico had never recognized Texas independence and border tensions had been brewing for years. With the Texas annexation under his belt, Polk moved on to preside over the acquisition of the vast Oregon Territory which extended American sovereignty to the Pacific in the north. But the issue of Texas and its claim of territory all the way to the Rio Grande were still on the table and would precipitate the Mexican War.

The military and diplomatic conduct of the war, although ultimately successful, was chaotic and marginally competent in its execution. Those terms also describe the process leading to the settlement of the conflict by the Treaty of Guadalupe Hidalgo. Communication between Washington and its military and diplomatic representatives in Mexico City was tortuously slow and confused. Further, General Winfield Scott, the American military leader, and Nicholas Trist, the President's designated treaty negotiator, were in open rebellion against the President.

Their behavior was so extreme that Polk finally attempted to recall Trist. Amazingly, Trist ignored the President's direct order and continued his negotiations with the Mexicans. He ultimately reached agreement with them on what would become the Treaty of Guadalupe Hidalgo. After much political warfare in Washington, the illegitimate treaty proved to meet the President's objectives. He reluctantly swallowed his pride and successfully pushed for final Congressional approval. The treaty was ultimately ratified by Mexico in 1848. The controversial war and the strangely crafted treaty added about 600,000 square miles of new territory and completed the American quest to own the Pacific coast from Mexico to Canada. Ironically, despite this gigantic mid century expansion of the American boundaries, the first Hispano settlement in what is now Colorado had still not been accomplished.

The Final Northern Frontier

I N THE TUMULTUOUS THREE DECADES from 1820 through the 1840s, New Mexico had passed from Spanish to Mexican and now to American control. With the end of the Mexican War, the San Luis Valley was part of the New Mexico Territory with an American Governor in Santa Fe. The Hispanic pioneers were poised to move into the valley but they were dealing with a new landlord. Under the Treaty of Guadalupe Hidalgo, the former Mexican citizens were to be protected in all their pre-existing property rights. The debate still rages about the extent to which the United States failed in its responsibility under the treaty, but we will only consider what happened to the land grants in the San Luis Valley.

There were two Mexican land grants and together they virtually blanketed the southern end of the valley. One, the Sangre de Cristo Grant, was to provide the legal basis for the first settlement in the valley and the first permanent village in what would become the state of Colorado. It was a huge 1,000,000 acre grant comprising land on the east side of the Rio Grande. Only parts of the grant would ultimately be confirmed. The part of the grant germane to the early settlement was along the Culebra and Costilla Rivers, tributaries of the Rio Grande.

The original grantees were Taos Sheriff Stephan Luis Lee and Narcisso Beaubien, son of a famous Taos character, Carlos Beaubien. Before any successful settlement attempt, the Mexican War intervened. Then, in 1847, there was an attempted uprising in Taos against the Americans by former Mexican citizens and their Taos Pueblo allies. In the course of this battle several citizens were killed including New Mexico Governor, Charles Bent and both of the grant holders. The revolt was quickly and brutally put down by the Americans.

The surviving father of one grantee, Carlos Beaubien, became the apparent sole owner of the grant, and in 1851 he selected colonists to settle on the culebra, near the Rio Grande in a place that became San Luis, Colorado. The village was designed to provide protection against Indian attack and although the Utes didn't give up easily, the village survived and even managed to sponsor several other plaza villages over the next few years.

The other grant brings us back to the southwestern part of the San Luis Valley. The Conejos Grant was made by Mexican Governor Francisco Serracino in 1833 to some forty families. The grant was never surveyed so its boundaries are uncertain. However, the Spanish description said that it was bounded on the north by Garita Hill, on the east by the east by the Rio Grande, on the west by the San Juan mountains and on the south by San Antonio Mountain. It included the Conejos River, the Rio San Antonio and the Rio de Los Pinos. There can be little doubt that the Santa Rita Canyon was within the grant boundaries as so described.

An early attempt at settlement in 1833 was thwarted by the Indians. In 1842, several of the original settlers including Jose Maria Martinez, Antonio Martinez, Julian Gallegos and Seledonio Valdez submitted the grant document to the Mexican authorities so that it could be revalidated. After approval, the local judicial official accompanied over 80 families to the banks of the Conejos River in October, 1842 for an elaborate ceremony to put them in possession of the land. Each family was given a strip of land extending from the Rio San Antonio in the south to the Rio La Jara in the north. Again, this attempt to perfect the grant by permanent settlement failed because of forceful opposition by the Ute Indians as the proposed village was in the heart of their homeland.

The Mexican War intervened and much of New Mexico was in turmoil. After the transfer of sovereignty was complete, the grantees approached the provisional governor of the Territory, Charles Bent, who was uncertain of his authority but gave his approval to another settlement effort in 1846. Again the attempt to settle was defeated.

In 1852 the Americans built Fort Massachusetts, the first frontier fort in the valley, at the edge of the Sangre de Cristo Mountains. Not long after that they established Fort Garland. Perhaps this new protection encouraged the pioneer New Mexicans who once more came north in 1854 to create the plaza village of Guadalupe on the north bank of the Conejos River. The community soon moved to a more suitable location on the south bank of the Conejos to create the new village called Conejos.

The people who came to this new village were New Mexico Hispanics but different historians have different views on their identity and places of origin. Luther E. Bean in *The Land of the Blue Sky People* says the grantees were Antonio Gallegos of El Rito and Julian Gallegos of Taos. Frances Mead in "Conejos County" says the persons named in the grant document were Jose Maria Martinez, Julian Gallegos, Atencio Martinez and Celedonio Valdez. Another leader in the creation of Conejos who became a lifelong resident was Colonel Lafayette Head. He served in the New Mexico territorial legislature and would later be a member of the Colorado territorial legislature, serving the same constituency. Whatever the truth may be about the details, a substantial number of New Mexico families committed themselves to building this community in the wilderness. The village was successful but the land grant upon which it was based continued to be disputed and litigated for decades and was ultimately completely rejected by the American courts.

Colville in her *La Vereda, A Trail through Time* said that after the successful start of Conejos, "many Spanish New Mexico families had established 'cordillera' or plaza farming settlements amid the lands watered by the rivers San Antonio, Los Pinos and Conejos...." Among them, she listed Lobatos, Cenicero, Cordón, El Codo, San Antonio, Ortiz, Los Pinos, Los Furecitos, Los Cerrillos, La Isla, Las Placitas, El Brazo, El Cedro, San Rafael, Bernalillo and Pura y Limpia.

The first government survey within the present boundaries of Colorado was made in the San Luis valley in the vicinity of Conejos in 1858 by A.P. Wilbar, deputy surveyor of New Mexico. His field notes mentioned "numerous Mexican settlements" in the area. Survey plats and early maps show Conejos, Servilleta, Brazoso, San Francisco, Cañon, Mazeta, and San Rafael all on the Conejos River and San Antonio on the Rio San Antonio.

In the two decades after the first permanent settlements in the valley, there was a veritable explosion of village building and construction of irrigation facilities especially in the lower reaches of all the tributary streams of the Rio Grande that flow through the valley. By the end of the 1860s, the period of Hispano colonization of the upper Rio Grande region was essentially complete, except for what might be called in fill settlements in the places that had been by passed in the northern surge. Those exceptions include the higher altitude upper reaches of mountain streams, such as the Rio de Los Pinos, where Hispano pioneers were still planting new villages and rancho communities, like Santa Rita, at the end of the nineteenth century and into the early twentieth century.

This description of the step by step northern advance of Hispano pioneers may make the process seem inevitable and foreordained but that would be for from the truth. Every step was dangerous and challenging. The colonists were moving into an increasingly hostile physical environment and were resisted at every stage by the Indian people whose territory they were invading. Even after the many settlements in the San Luis valley were successfully established the region was still a war zone and would continue to be until late in the nineteenth century.

Any review of the conflict between the Utes and the Hispano pioneers would be incomplete without mentioning the role of Christopher Houston Carson. Kit Carson was already the hero of dime novels by mid century. He was only forty years old in 1850 but had made a name for himself as a trapper, hunter and as a guide and scout for better known explorers. He had married Josefa Jaramillo, an Hispana woman from a prominent Taos family and had taken up ranching and working as a scout for the army.

In 1854 he became an Indian Agent for several tribes including the Utes and played a major role in trying to settle the growing number of disputes between them and the settlers in San Luis valley.

The place of the genízaro people in borderland society was mentioned earlier. Kit Carson's family is an example of the way things were done. Church records in Taos show the baptism of three Navajos " in the charge of Cristobal Carson" in 1860 and 1864. (Tom Dunlay, *Kit Carson and the Indians*) One of them is reported to have been ransomed from the Utes in 1858. Kit Carson's son, Christopher, in later years told the story (also from Dunlay):

A party of Utes came along from a fight with Navajos. A three-year-old boy of that tribe had been captured. The Ute chief told mother that the boy was a bother to them and they intended to kill him. She knew an appeal for his life would be useless so she asked what they would sell him for. A horse was named as the price, which mother immediately gave them and took the boy into our home. Later father adopted him and gave him the name of Juan Carson.

During the late 1850s there were frequent Ute-Hispano confrontations that Carson attempted to mediate in his capacity as agent. The Utes were being gradually displaced by the settlers and the mutual antagonism was growing. One incident occurred in 1859 near the village of San Antonio, just north of what is now the New Mexico-Colorado line and just down river from Los Pinos. A Ute man had made the mistake of picking an ear of corn from a settler's field. Carson's report to his superior stated (Dunlay):

They had a few words and clinched, the Mexican was stabbed pretty severely in the back by an arrow, the Mexican then got a club and beat the Indian, from the effects of which he will in all probability die... The Indians immediately commenced surrounding fully armed, an express was sent for me I immediately proceeded to the place of difficulty and found them much enraged and I do believe if I had not gone the Indians would have massacred all in town.

Kit Carson continues to be a controversial figure even today, remembered by some as a hero and by others as a villain. By today's standards it would be difficult to defend his role in the defeat of the Navajos and their horrendous "Long Walk" to the Bosque Redondo on the Pecos River in the 1860s or some of his actions in the Indian wars.

But it is also true that he was often a friend and protector of the Indians and a vocal critic of the worst abuses perpetrated by the army. He roundly condemned Col. John Chivington for his notorious role in the Sand Creek

Massacre of the Cheyennes in 1864. "... Jist to think of that dog Chivington, and his dirty hounds, up thar at Sand Creek! Whoever heerd of sich doings 'mong Christians!" His sympathy for the Indians was clear: "... Pore things! Pore things! I've seen as much of them as any man liv'n, and I can't help but pity 'em, ... They once owned all this country yes, Plains and Mountains, buffalo and everything, but now they own next to nothing, and soon will be gone." (Dunley) He must be seen as a man of his time and the most extreme negative and positive stereotypes are probably inaccurate.

Soon after the establishment of the Hispano presence in the San Luis Valley, the discovery of gold in the north brought a new wave of Anglo treasure hunters and settlers to Colorado and Mormon farmers soon arrived to compete for land in the valley. The Ute Indians were under siege by all the new comers. They were forced to the bargaining table with little bargaining power and signed several treaties between the 1850s and the 1880s that had the net result of extinguishing their rights to the land of the valley and ultimately forcing their removal to reservations in southwest Colorado and southeast Utah.

By the 1860s the plaza communities on both sides of the valley were thriving and expanding. In 1860, Colorado became a separate territory and the northern boundary of New Mexico was established essentially where it is today. Rapid development occurred in much of Colorado, precipitated in large part by the discovery of precious metals. But agricultural settlers were also aggressively taking up land in the San Luis Valley and elsewhere in the region. Many of the new farmers were Anglo newcomers who over time became the dominant presence in the easily domesticated lands along the major streams in the area. Hispano pioneers, including Seledon Valdez, one of the original members of the Conejos Land Grant, were also among those establishing new homesteads, but they were in the minority among the larger property owners. The growth of Colorado's Anglo population contributed to political pressure for statehood and the territory became a state in 1876. The overwhelming Hispano and Catholic majority in New Mexico was a negative factor in the eyes of national political leaders that delayed New Mexico statehood until well into the twentieth century.

In 1862, the Congress passed the original Homestead Act and many of the Hispano settlers began using the new law to acquire property in New Mexico and the new Colorado territory. Ironically, many users of the Homestead process were probably people who would have been entitled to property rights under the Conejos land grant if it had been recognized by American authorities.

Rio De Los Pinos Settlements

B Y EARLY IN THE 1860s, much of the prime land in the Conejos region had been occupied by the new settlers. We know from Kit Carson's 1859 report that there was already a settlement on the Colorado border called San Antonio. This small plaza village was on the banks of the Rio San Antonio, just downstream from its confluence with the Rio de Los Pinos. At the time, San Antonio was still in New Mexico. After the flurry of early Hispanic settlement in the Conejos area, the more aggressive and sophisticated Anglo settlers began to acquire the larger and more easily developed agricultural lands further north in the San Luis Valley. They were more likely to have the financial capacity required for the extensive irrigation infrastructure that was necessary to serve larger farms. As a result, many Hispano pioneers began to look to the higher country at the southern end of the San Luis Valley. They were still following the rivers north but their options were becoming more limited because of the land rush in the lower valley and further north in Colorado. So, they began to consider the more challenging undeveloped upstream prospects on the Rio de Los Pinos.

We know from 1850 and 1860 census reports that some of the Hispanic people who originally settled the Conejos area were beginning to move back to Rio Arriba County. Then, repeating the historical pattern of "contiguous expansion", they stepped out from places like San Antonio, moving west and up river to places that would be called Ortiz and Los Pinos and later, San Miguel.

There was both continuity and change in the nature of these Hispano people who were repeating the ancient patterns of settlement in the late nineteenth century and even into the early twentieth century. During the two hundred and fifty years before 1850, they had evolved culturally and genetically. They still asserted their Spanish identity, sometimes describing themselves as Españoles Mexicanos. A majority of them could be described as mestizos, having incorporated the blood of Mexican and American Indians. The genízaro people were now also a part of the mix, bringing with them the blood of many plains and other nomadic Indian tribes.

Culturally, the Hispano people had left their mark on their homeland with their villages, their notched log, adobe and jacal houses, their churches, their acequias and the other elements of their Spanish cultural heritage. Out of necessity and choice, as they moved north, they tended to be herdsmen rather than farmers, which would serve them well along the small streams and narrow canyons in the high country. They shared DNA with their distant relatives in Spain and Mexico, but as a people they were very different. They were energetic and creative colonizers. They were adventurous risk takers and were quick to adapt to the new northern environment that was quite different from what they had experienced in the core of the old Santa Fe based homeland.

Their distance from remote centers of government and religious authority was both a challenge and a source of strength. They received little support from the government in Santa Fe and beyond and also had to be more self reliant in their religious lives, using the self administered rituals of the Penitente tradition. In contrast to their Mexican and Spanish ancestors, they were resistant to top down authoritarian direction and more inclined to independence and entrepreneurial spirit.

These Hispano pioneers were to be among the last to carry on the centuries old adventure of pushing the border of their homeland to the north along all the many rivers and streams that were the essential basis for their way of life. These little communities in the north were a final expression of the centuries long process of expanding the Hispano Homeland and it is only fitting that it should happen here along the Rio de Los Pinos, at the northern edge of Rio Arriba County.

When Stephan Watts Kearney occupied New Mexico in August, 1846, he promulgated a set of statutory laws that became known as the Kearney Code. The Code established local governments in the territory. The original seven counties were Rio Arriba, Taos, San Miguel del Abado, Santa Fe, Santa Ana, Bernalillo and Valencia. The counties of Soccoro and Doña

Ana were soon added. The western boundaries of several counties extended to the California border because the Arizona Territory had not yet been created. Originally, Taos County was a narrow strip along the northern edge of the territory, stretching from Texas to California, and included Conejos and other parts of southern Colorado. Rio Arriba County was just to its south, and its western border briefly extended to California.

At the time of the 1860 census, the Conejos area was still in Taos County but soon thereafter the borders were adjusted and Rio Arriba became the northernmost county on the west side of the Rio Grande while Taos County abutted Colorado on the east side. Colorado became a separate territory in 1860 and Arizona was separated from New Mexico in 1863. When Rio Arriba County was established, the county seat was Los Luceros. In 1852, the Legislature moved the county headquarters to San Pedro de Chamita and it remained there until 1860 when it was moved to Alcalde. It stayed there for the next tumultuous twenty years during which there was a gold and silver boom in the San Juan Mountains of Colorado. An interesting perspective on the rush for precious metals is provided by an addendum to the 1870 census. The enumerator was an agent for Indian Services in New Mexico but he conducted a census of miners on "the Utah Indian Reservation in Colorado Territory." He listed twenty five men, all Anglos, and added this intriguing note:

> 25 miners in the San Juan Indian Country ... over two hundred have been driven out by the Indians on whose land the mines are located ... The mines on this reservation are very valuable but owing to the Indian's claims to the land it can not be worked ... The Indians are willing to dispose of the mining region for cows and sheep.

So the Hispanos were not the only ones to suffer at the hands of the newcomers!

In 1880, there was a big change in Rio Arriba County. The legislature redrew the boundaries, giving much of western Taos County to Rio Arriba. The same law also moved the county seat to a small new village near the

Colorado line, called Las Nutritas. The same legislature also changed the name of that village to Tierra Amarillo.

It should come as no surprise that there was controversy about both the move and the name change. Contemporary observers said neither could not have happened without the involvement of Thomas D. Burns and his wife's family. Burns was a prominent Rio Arriban and his wife was Doña Josefa Gallegos, who came from another influential local family.

In 1887, the new county of San Juan was created out of the western part of Rio Arriba County. The county has had essentially the same boundaries since that time. So Rio Arriba's county seat was born in controversy and controversy has never been far from the scene since then.

Census records are among the few documentary sources of early history in the Rio de Los Pinos neighborhood. The first American census was in 1850, just before Hispano settlers ventured into the southern San Luis Valley. At that time, the newly created Taos County stretched all across the top of New Mexico and included what would become southern Colorado.

The Taos County census was conducted by Charles Williams who had the exalted title of "Assistant to the Marshall of New Mexico." There was only one geographic designation called the Northern Division and its population was listed as about 9,500 people, most of whom lived in the old part of the county, near the village of Taos. That 1850 count included only a handful of non- Hispanic names. Among them were Christopher Carson and his wife Maria Josefa Jaramillo. Their household included their one year old son, Charles B. Carson, and four other young people called Francisco Bueno, Melitona Anaya, Maria Luisa Shehicano and Juliana Jones. Some if not all of these people were probably genízaro members of the Carson family. Another interesting entry in the census is a man whose name is actually listed as "Hilario Captivo." In many instances young family members are listed with "Indian Country" as their places of birth and "Copper" as their race or color. The census also includes Charles Beaubien, a name we have heard before. It will be recalled that Carlos Beaubien, as he was better known, was the father of Narcisso Beaubien, one of the grantees of the Sangre de Cristo Grant. During the 1847 Taos uprising against the

Americans, many people were killed including Charles Bent, New Mexico's first territorial governor, and Narcisso Beaubien. Carlos Beaubien would later lead the journey north by the settlers who founded the village of San Luis in 1851.

Mr. Williams, the Anglo enumerator of the 1850 census, probably anglicized the first names of Carson and Beaubien, who were better known by the Spanish version of their given names. Another intriguing name in the census is that of Teodoro Wheaton, a lawyer, who was born in Rhode Island. Wheaton's mother would surely have been surprised to learn that her son's given name was "Teodoro"! Carson, Beaubien, Wheaton and the few other Anglo men in the census, were, with rare exceptions, married to Hispana women and were fully incorporated into the dominant Hispano culture. In Carson's case, notwithstanding his Kentucky and Missouri beginnings, he was probably more fluent in Spanish than in English.

The 1860 Taos County census includes four districts described as "Townships No.16, 17, 18 and 19 of Conejos." The record doesn't describe the location of the four "townships" but they must Include the several plaza villages that had sprung up in the area since Conejos (Guadalupe) was settled in 1854. The census reported about 230 households in the Conejos "townships." Lafayette Head, one of the founders of Guadalupe, appeared in the census. His household of ten, included three persons identified by race as "IND." and another described as a "servant." Their places of birth were "unknown." All four were probably genízaros. The 1860 census does not tell us how many families may have been living south of the line that would soon become the New Mexico-Colorado border, but it seems likely that there must have been a few.

The 1870 census removes all doubt. It contains a division called "The Town of Pinos." The enumerator listed eighty two families living there. Among them, six children, in four different families, were described as "Indians" and in each case their occupation was shown as "domestic." These six young people were almost certainly genízaros and there are probably others in the community who were so well integrated that they were not differentiated from their blood relatives.

It seems likely that these 1870 families lived in both the "town" of Los Pinos and in the dispersed community that ventured out to the edge of the village and upstream along the Rio de Los Pinos. In this area, the river passes through broad meadows and provided the potential for irrigated farming and stock grazing. It is interesting to note that while there were some eighty families in the "Town of Pinos," there were only thirty two different family names. Among the names appearing most frequently are Martinez, Gallegos, Archuleta, Duran, Espinosa, Sisneros and Lucero.

During the 1870s, there was rapid growth throughout the region, especially in the north where the engine of American migration and development was most pronounced. Many new towns and even young cities emerged and by the end of the decade the railroad had entered Colorado. The Anglo population had grown to the extent that in 1876, Colorado was granted statehood, unlike its sister territory New Mexico, which would have to wait until 1912. When Colorado became a state, its capital city Denver was already a boom town.

An 1879 map of New Mexico that also depicts southern Colorado features, shows many new towns in Colorado including Pueblo, Trinidad, Walsenburgh, Canon City and Saguache. The same map also shows some of the villages at the southern edge of Colorado including Conejos, San Antonio, San Rafael and San Jose. It doesn't show any villages on the New Mexico side of the line although the 1870 census suggests that settlement had begun in that area. That map shows the proposed route of the Denver and Rio Grande Railroad (D&RG) running south through the San Luis Valley, and with grand ambition, all the way down through New Mexico to a dead end in the boot heel area south of Silver City.

The railroad would have a big impact on the lives of people in the valley. The Denver and Rio Grande Railway Company was chartered in 1870 with a route south from Denver planned to extend all the way to El Paso. That never happened but the line reached Pueblo in 1872, La Veta in 1876 and the new town of Alamosa in 1878. After some litigation caused delays, construction was restarted and the railroad reached the new company town of Antonito in 1880.

From Antonito, the line divided, one route going south to Española, the other heading west through the rugged San Juan Mountains, past the Toltec Gorge, over Cumbres Pass to another railroad town to be known as Chama. The western track ran parallel to the upper Rio de Los Pinos, overlooking the place where the tiny settlement called Santa Rita was soon to be born.

The 1880 census for Rio Arriba County is something of a mystery in that it seems to show fewer families in the Los Pinos precinct than did the 1870 census. The "enumeration description" includes Los Pinos, San Antonito and San Antonito Arriba, but provides no guidance from which we can plot exact locations. The approximately thirty families were probably spread out from the village of Los Pinos to undetermined locations up the Rio de Los Pinos valley. The mystery may be partially explained by the rapid growth of its immediate Colorado neighbor, Ortiz. This thriving village was right on the border and was reported to have a population of about five hundred people in 1880. The 1880 census introduced a new category of occupation. In addition to the traditional farmers, farm laborers, sheep owners, sheep herders, schoolmasters, weavers and washerwomen we also see a few railroad laborers listed. At the end of the census, the enumerator added the following hand written note:

> In this part of my district are no farms wich (sic) give a production of 500 Dollars per anum, people is more interested in sheepraising, and raise only little crops of wheat. Settled about 2 or 3 years ago.

This suggests that by the late 1870s, the Hispano people had not yet moved up the valley to the site of the village of San Miguel. That event would wait until sometime in the early 1880s. Another footnote to the 1880 census is an unexplained small enumeration category called "Tollgate." It must have been nearby since it was recorded by the same enumerator. The history of the D&RG Railroad reveals that the route towards the Cumbres Pass was close to what was described as the Parkview and Conejos Toll Road, which was apparently used by the D&RG to transport equipment and supplies for the western extension. That may account for the "Tollgate" census, which reported three families there. The tollgate keeper, W. E. Wilson and his wife, were from Vermont and New York. The "Teamster," William Snyder and his wife, were from Kansas and Maryland and the "tollroad laborer" and his wife, were from Indiana. The tollgate Community also included two Hispano laborers and a Hispana cook, all from New Mexico.

The Hispano pioneers had not yet ventured upstream to Santa Rita Canyon at the beginning of the 1880s but the railroad was already there. Just walking distance up the canyon side from where they would settle, was a little station and work camp called Sublette, still used as a watering station today by the Cumbres and Toltec Scenic Railway. The track was completed to Sublette in the fall of 1880. It is recorded that by October of that year there were about one hundred people living there in tents and frame shacks. This temporary camp community served as the staging area for the crews laying track west towards Chama.

The decade of the 1880s was pivotal to the upriver expansion from Los Pinos to San Miguel and ultimately into Santa Rita Canyon. The distance from Los Pinos to San Miguel is over four miles and in much of that stretch of the river, the canyon is narrow and provided little potential for farming. In the San Miguel neighborhood the valley widens and there were good conditions for home building and irrigated farming. And that is what the Hispano settlers began to do in that decade.

Above San Miguel, the canyon is again a narrow passage between steep cliffs for about four miles until it opens up to wide meadows with good irrigation prospects at the lower end of Santa Rita Canyon. Records are sketchy but it seems likely that by the late 1880s, the first pioneers were establishing their homesteads, planting crops, building acequias and grazing their stock in that area.

One reason for the lack of evidence of settlement is that the census of 1890 is missing. The census was conducted but a fire in the Commerce Department building in Washington, DC in 1920, destroyed the only known copy of the population schedules for all of New Mexico. Therefore it is difficult to accurately gauge the population of the small but growing communities along the upper Rio de Los Pinos. Fortunately, other records including recorded real estate documents tell us something about the extent of settlement.

Applications for homestead entries and the issuance of patents confirm that by the late 1880s the first settlers were venturing into Santa Rita Canyon. This five mile segment of the river was the last place on the river that was suitable even for subsistence farming. At the head of the valley, the river tumbles down about thousand feet through the Toltec Gorge. This marks the end of the line for viable agricultural living. It was in this high mountain valley that these hardy people initiated homesteads in the last years of the nineteenth century and the early years of the twentieth century

These adventurers were certainly among the last participants in the three hundred year long journey to expand the Hispano Homeland. To the very end they followed the rivers north and pursued their precarious way of life. And even at the beginning of the twentieth century, that way of life didn't differ significantly from what it had been for their ancestors. It appears that all the first landowners in Santa Rita acquired their land titles under the provisions of the Homestead Act. The earliest patents were issued in the early years of the twentieth century. However, it is clear that the people began moving in much earlier without benefit of legal ownership of their land. One homesteader, Jose Bacilio Duran stated in his final proof testimony that he had established "actual residence" on the property in 1888 and built his house in the same year. But the patent was not issued until 1911, twenty three years later. The same pattern appears in several other homestead files.

All the Santa Rita patents were for lands within the Carson National Forest, but the Forest did not officially come into existence until 1908, by Executive Order of President Theodore Roosevelt. Amazingly, President Roosevelt, called "The Wilderness Warrior" by one of his biographers, by the stroke of his pen, created one hundred fifty national forests during his time in office. All the homesteaders in Santa Rita were Hispanos and it appears that they used the Homestead Act to validate their de facto ownership, established on the ground by occupancy at an earlier and less formal time.

But step back and observe the trend of change in the Los Pinos, San Miguel and Santa Rita neighborhood. The 1900 census for the Los Pinos district shows a population of about four hundred fifty and about one hundred fifteen families. No geographic break down of the district was provided.

In 1910, there were over 730 people listed in Precinct 15. A marginal note indicated that the precinct covered the area described as "Los Pinos Main Road from the northern boundary of N. Mex. to Los Crestones." The name " Los Crestones" appears without definition in several plats and maps of that period. It probably refers to giant rocky prominences in Santa Rita Canyon, visible from most of the upper valley. These land features probably marked the upper limit of settlement in 1910. We will later have more to say about Los Crestones.

In 1920, the census for precinct 15 (Los Pinos) recorded forty eight families and a total population of three hundred twenty. The census was divided into descriptive segments, the uppermost being "Santa Rita Main Road." Even today that road is a rough, four wheel drive track. Calling it a "Main Road" in 1920 must have been a real euphemism.

This last segment of the census includes families who were among the first homesteaders in Santa Rita. The microfilm copy of the census is very unclear and difficult to read and some of the names are illegible. To complete the census record for the Los Pinos Valley, we turn to the listings for 1930, which is the latest census for which detailed population data is available at the time of this writing.

The enumerator's description of the "township or other division of the county" is ambiguous. The first two pages include eighty nine people in nineteen families and at the bottom of the second page, the following notation appears: "Here ends San Miguel Township." The last page records thirty three people in eight families and concludes with this notation: "Here ends Santa Rita Township."

This record shows a population trend for the Los Pinos area starting at four hundred forty five in 1900, increasing to over seven hundred in 1910 and decreasing to two hundred fifty in 1920 and one hundred twenty two in

1930. It is likely that the population peaked in Santa Rita sometime during the two decades between 1910 and 1930.

Later we will see that declining population was a wide spread phenomenon at this time, similar to what was happening throughout rural America at the same time. The world was catching up with the Hispano pioneers as they began the process of integrating into the broader American society. But at this outer edge of the dominant American society, the changes were not very obvious. Their community continued to be culturally homogeneous and their way of life had not altered dramatically.

We now have a rough picture of how the valley looked in the early years of the twentieth century, but how does it look a hundred years later? The physical place looks very much the same. The beautiful river still runs through the narrow canyons, edged by wide meadows, with willows and mountain cottonwoods on its banks. Looking up from the valley floor, one sees mountains sprinkled with ponderosa pines and aspen groves. From many points along the river a viewer can still watch the coal smoke and listen to the steam whistle of the old narrow gauge Denver and Rio Grande Railroad, now called the Cumbres and Toltec Scenic Railroad. The treacherous "Santa Rita Main Road" still runs five miles up the valley, accessing about fifteen cabins and small houses.

However much the place looks the same, everything else has changed. The Hispano community of Santa Rita began to fade away over sixty years ago. The descendants of one Santa Rita homesteader family still farm and graze their cattle in the valley, but their primary residence is now over the mountains to the north in the village of Mogote, Colorado. Many of the other old families saw some of their sons leave the homesteads in the middle of the twentieth century to find work in the mines or on the large farms in the San Luis Valley or to pursue other opportunities in the larger outside world. They became a part of the restless American migratory mainstream, moving always westward to Arizona, California and beyond. Some families moved down river to the villages and small towns in the San Luis Valley where their grandparents or great grandparents had lived in the late 1800s.

When the people left, homestead by homestead, they sold their places to a new kind of seekers and searchers. These new people didn't come here to make a living. Perhaps they could be called lifestyle pioneers. They came for the beauty of the place and to enjoy the peace and quiet at the edge of the wilderness. They came for the fishing and hunting and to enjoy vicariously, without serious pain or struggle, the rigorous life of the real pioneers.

And of course they were all part timers and with few exceptions Anglos. They were lawyers, doctors, large scale farmers, business people, bankers and retired folks. When they were not enjoying their places in Santa Rita, they lived in places like Santa Fe, Las Cruces, Albuquerque, Taos, Colorado, Arizona, Oklahoma and California.

The newcomers appreciate those who came before them. They enjoy learning about the Hispano and Indian history of the area. They are conscious of the connection their Hispano neighbors still feel for Santa Rita and the other Los Pinos River valley villages. Their understanding of that connection is strengthened by their friendship with their neighbors Baudelio and Arlene Garcia. Baudelio's great grandfather and grandfather were homesteaders in the valley. The Garcias still live part of their lives in Santa Rita. In their early married years they lived year round in the valley. His parents' home was an old adobe house, probably built by one of the homesteader families and later acquired by Baudelio's parents, Antonio and Juanita Garcia. The Garcia family often used the unoccupied house next door for its extra bedrooms. That house was owned by the Archuleta family but was unoccupied after the father, Francisco, died in the early 1930s and the rest of the family moved down river or, in the case of the sons, went north to work in the mines. After their marriage, Baudelio and Arlene lived and started to raise their two children in the old adobe house on the next homestead down the road, that had been owned by another family member and was subsequently bought by the senior Garcias. Baudelio later became the owner of that house and he and Arlene lived there until they made the move to Mogote. The old people continued to live in their old place until they were unable to stay there on their own and moved to Antonito. They still used their house in Santa Rita on a seasonal basis until their deaths and loved to be in the valley during the gentle days of summer.

The younger Garcias divided their time between Mogote and Santa Rita. They worked the land in both places, irrigating the Santa Rita land, cutting and baling hay and grazing their cattle there and in the National Forest, where Baudelio had grazing permits. They no longer had full time neighbors in the valley, although there was still a lively social scene in the larger neighborhood, made accessible first by horses and buggies and later by the internal combustion engine.

So, the Garcias became part timers. Even their cattle went over the northern hills each autumn to spend the winters in Mogote. When the Garcias were in Santa Rita, they often had it all to themselves, as the other "locals" were usually far away in their other world. In the absence of full time residents, the valley was empty of people during the long winters, and quietly rested under a blanket of deep snow, disturbed only by the tracks of the elk, deer and other native creatures.

There will be more to say about the contemporary Santa Rita and the local descendants of the early homesteaders. But for now we return to finish the story of the creation of what the census enumerator grandly described as "Santa Rita Township."

The Old Places of Santa Rita

A SEARCH OF BUREAU of Land Management records and other old documents reveals that there were twelve homestead patents in Santa Rita Canyon. The homestead locations are depicted on the "Homestead Map."

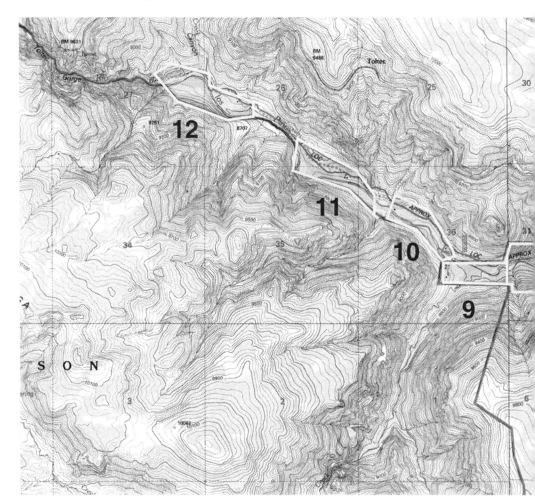

Santa Rita Homestead Map

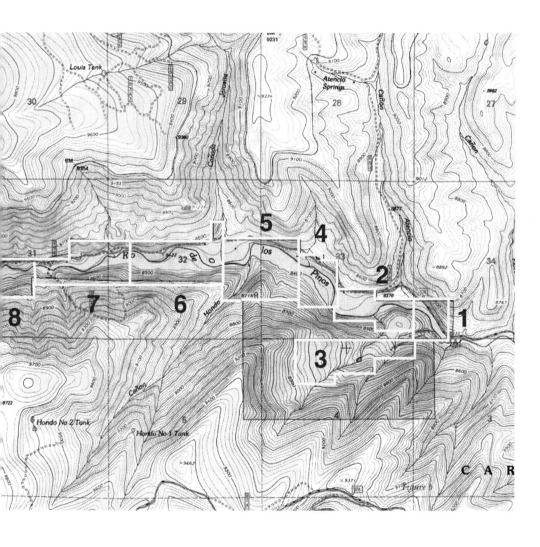

The map is derived from United States Geological Survey quadrangles for "Toltec Mesa" and "Big Horn Peak." The numbered tracts roughly outline the boundaries of the twelve homesteads.

The following list provides the names of the original homesteaders by tract number:

1. Juan C. Cisneros
2. Jose Nestor Ruybalid
3. Polito Garcia (Hipolito)
4. Juan Bautista Gallegos
5. Jose Bacilio Duran
6. Juan de Dios Duran
7. Maximo Quintana (Maximiliano)
8. Antonio Duran
9. J. Luciano Tafoya
10. Albino Duran
11. Felix Martinez
12. Emilio Martinez

While most of the settlers were married with families, the patents were always issued to the men in the families.

As the map shows, the community of Santa Rita extends from Atencio Canyon in the east to the last homestead, just below Toltec Gorge, in the west. All the land outside the solid line homestead boundaries is in the Carson National Forest. From homestead number eight on to the west, the land south of the homesteads is now part of the Cruces Basin Wilderness Area.

The records available do not make it possible to pin point actual dates of original occupancy by most of the settlers. As previously noted, we know from contemporary observations that in many cases the pioneer settlers moved onto the land without benefit of legal process Then sometime later, frequently many years later, they validated their de facto ownership by pursuing homestead patents. We also know little about the order in which the homesteads were physically occupied.

The first place above the narrow canyon to the east of Santa Rita was acquired by Juan C. Cisneros. His forty acre patent was issued in 1912. He may have arrived later than some of his upstream neighbors. The second place was also patented in 1912 to Jose Nestor Ruybalid, and included seventy acres. This land later passed to Baudelio Garcia's uncle, Daniel Gallegos, then to his mother, Juanita Garcia and ultimately to Baudelio Garcia. It is still part of his Santa Rita ranch.

An early survey, probably in 1908, provides a visual picture of the canyon. The surveyor described the steep terrain and the trees and brush he had to struggle through to do his work, frequently mentioning groves of "quakenasp" which must refer to the still ubiquitous aspen trees. He said the river was "80 links wide" in July, referring to the chain which was one of the surveyor's tools. He also mentioned a landmark described as "Crestonis, a massive volcanic rock, 1000 feet high." It will be recalled that Los Crestones was the geographic reference in the 1910 census, marking the western extent of settlement in that year. Ruben Cobos' *Dictionary of New Mexico and Southern Colorado Spanish* describes "creston" as "highest top or summit." That definition neatly fits two dominant geologic features in the valley. One is what is known today as "Maxie's Mountain" named after Maximo Quintana, a homesteader who will be discussed later. Nearby is another high, rocky outcrop. These two peaks must be "Los Crestones" referred to in the census.

Los Crestones. This photograph shows irrigated meadows
and the two distinctive summits.

Typical homestead cabin, Santa Rita, New Mexico.

The third homestead of 131 acres was in steep rugged terrain across the river and was patented to Polito Garcia in 1917. He was listed as Hipolito Garcia in the 1920 census. His son, Antonio, was Baudelio Garcia's father. Family relationships in Santa Rita were complicated and frequently interconnected, so it should be no surprise that Antonio Garcia was the grandson of the next homesteader.

We know quite a bit about the Juan Bautista Gallegos family because of genealogical research done by members of the Garcia family. Juan Gallegos was married in 1875 to Abelina Ruybalid who was born in Ojo Caliente, New Mexico in 1857. Juan and Abelina appear in the 1910, 1920 and 1930 Los Pinos Census enumerations, so it is clear that they were long time residents. Gallegos received his patent for fifty acres in 1912, but he and his family had certainly been there well before that date. He shared acequias on both sides of the river with upstream and downstream neighbors who, in time, would be the Garcia family as they ultimately acquired the property both east and west of him.

The original owner of the next property above the Gallegos family was another old timer, who may have been the first settler in that area. Jose Bacilio Duran received his patent for one hundred twenty acres in 1911. But we have copies of his patent application papers that show he was on the land much earlier. Duran and his patent application witnesses claim that his actual occupancy began in 1888, so twenty three years passed between his arrival and the issuance of the patent. At the time he was making his final proof on the homestead he was thirty four years old. His father, Manuel Duran, who lived with him, was about seventy five years old, which suggests he was born in about 1835, well before the arrival of the Americans. The 1870 census for an area in Rio Arriba County called "Precinct #3, Vallecitos" included a Manuel Duran, aged 39, who could well be the same man. It is striking to think of the changes experienced by Manuel Duran, whose life spanned the Mexican and Territorial periods and ended after New Mexico became a state.

The Duran documents claim fifteen acres of cultivable land with seven to ten acres planted each year in potatoes, oats and wheat. He said, "I also have about 1,000 head of sheep grazing there, they belong to Frederico Warshaw, I have them on shares." That arrangement, called "partidos" in Spanish, was a common practice by which poorer settlers could acquire their own sheep by caring for the flocks of their more prosperous neighbors.

Frederico Warshaw was in fact Fred Warshaw, a German immigrant who arrived in the San Luis Valley sometime in the 1880s. He originally settled in Conejos where he was in the real estate and loan business. He was quite successful and moved to the new town of Antonito where he continued to thrive in the sheep and wool business. He and the other well to do ranchers and business people built large houses on the Anglo side of town. "The Warshaw Mansion" is still there and still imposing in a town of small houses. Unfortunately, Warshaw reportedly fell on hard times and is said to have committed suicide in 1913. He was one of numerous German immigrants, many of them Jews, who were among the new mercantile elite in northern New Mexico and southern Colorado.

Jose Duran listed improvements including a five room house, corrals, stable with hay room and fencing. A September, 1910 letter from Forest Ranger H. F. Wade, reported that Duran had twenty five acres in cultivation (oats, barley, potatoes) with "20 acres under ditch, producing 5-10 tons of hay each year and 5,000 to 15,000 pounds of potatoes per year."

It is interesting to consider that all the documents required in the homesteading process were created in the English language and almost all of the participants in the process were Spanish speakers with virtually no English language skills. In most cases they were also unable to read or write in either language and signed their documents with an "X." It must have been an adventure to deal with such unfamiliar processes, in a foreign language and with the uncertain help of people who were not you friends and confidants. It was a circumstance that greatly disadvantaged Hispano people all over the north.

After a series of conveyances, the Duran land came to be owned by Antonio and Juanita Garcia. Over the course of years there was at least one tax sale to the state for unpaid taxes of $69, probably the amount due for many years of taxes. The tax and penalties were paid and the property was recovered. It was not uncommon to see records of sales for as little as less than ten dollars in unpaid taxes. Coming to grips with the cash economy was a challenge in many Hispano villages all over northern New Mexico.

The next homesteader was Jose Bacilio Duran's brother Juan de Dios Duran, whose eighty five acres were patented in 1911. He moved to the property in 1897 and built his four room house at that time. Most of the homestead houses were made from notched logs plastered with adobe mud inside and outside. We have a picture of an early twentieth century house, abandoned nearly seventy five years ago, that is typical of the settlers' first homes. They usually had three or four rooms, all in a row. Sometimes they were of jacal construction in which the walls were made with vertical, side by side cedar or ponderosa posts, set into the ground and rising to roof height and adobe plastered as described above. There were also some conventional adobe brick houses but they were less common. The local forest provided good quality logs and it was difficult and time consuming to make and cure adobe bricks. Some houses had smooth earthen floors. It was also common to lay vigas (beams) on the ground as a foundation for rough hewn wooden floors.

The physical logistics of homesteading were challenging. At the time of these proceedings, Santa Rita was a small, remote orphan community in Rio Arriba County. The county seat was in Tierra Amarilla, about a hundred wagon road miles away.

A striking example of how hard it was to get the job done is found in the Juan de Dios Duran file. He missed an appointment with a local official in Tierra Amarilla in January, 1911. An affidavit filed a few days later tells the story: "Juan D. Duran …says he did not appear before the probate clerk on the 12th day of January, A.D. … on account of the train being delayed on account of snow storm raging over the mountains on that date and the day after." One can only imagine the three or four day journey required to get to Tierra Amarillo and back. If he was living on his homestead he might have climbed up through the deep snow to Sublette on the Denver and Rio Grande Railroad track or perhaps he found his way to Antonito to catch the train to Chama. On arriving there, he still had a difficult trip on rough roads for another fifteen miles to the court house in Tierra Amarilla. And when the business was taken care of he faced the same arduous trip home.

In the second quarter of the twentieth century, Juan D. Duran's land was owned at various times by Baudelio Garcia's brothers Santiago and Octaviano and by Alfonso Marquez. The property was irrigated by a north side acequia that had its headgate on the Juan Duran land but also served the Jose Duran, Juan Gallegos and Jose Ruybalid acreage. Other acequias on the south side of the Rio de Los Pinos also watered multiple properties and there were numerous other ditches on up the valley. Unlike many of the community acequias in the older villages of northern New Mexico, these did not have formal organizations with elected mayordomos and rules of operation but they required the same collective effort to construct, maintain and operate.

In addition to the main stream source, irrigation water was also provided by small intermittent streams like Cañada Jarosita and Cañon Hondo that contributed strong flows to the river and fields in the spring and early summer. Further up stream at the property homesteaded by J. Luciano Tafoya, Lobo Creek flows down out of the magnificent 18,000 acre Cruces Basin Wilderness into the Rio de Los Pinos. The Lobo Creek and its tributaries bring water down from elevations of over 10,000 feet and drain some of the grandest aspen groves and spruce forests in all of New Mexico.

Max Quintana was forty three years old when he made his final proof and received his patent on one hundred acres in 1913. His given name had evolved over the years. In the 1910 census he was Maximiliano. In 1920, he was Maximo and in 1930, he was Max. We know the location of his three room house and out buildings built in 1903, but even the ruins have long since disappeared. The property was divided frequently among family and in laws and another house built by his son, Modesto, still survives in close to its original shape.

Maximo is reputed to have been a famous New Mexico game warden. It must have been an interesting occupation in an area so out of reach of conventional law enforcement. People living in Santa Rita at the time say that there were virtually no game animals in the valley at that time. They had been hunted out and were just beginning to recover. By the end of the twentieth century all the original species were abundant and the beavers were always happy to dam the river and block the acequias.

The river canyon above Quintana is narrow and the slopes are steep on both sides of the river. The canyon is always in the shadow of towering ponderosa pines. Despite the challenge, that stretch of river and the more open area above it became part of Antonio Duran's homestead. His patent, issued in 1919, included about ninety acres. We don't know when he settled there or where his house was located. The 1930 census showed him to be fifty seven years old. He is listed as a widower with six children living with him. There were five daughters and one son, Austerberto, who was nine years old at that time. His son inherited the property and was the owner until the late 1940s when he deeded it to one of the first Anglos to acquire land in Santa Rita.

The adjoining up stream property was a thirty nine acre homestead acquired by J. Luciano Tafoya in 1927. By 1930, he was seventy one years old and living with his son, Tranquilino, and family. Tranquilino sold the property in 1946 to the same newcomer who had bought the Antonio Duran place. The current owner still uses a rustic cabin that may have been the original Tafoya homestead.

Just up hill and up steam form the Tafoya place is the Albino Duran homestead. His patent for over forty five acres was dated 1917, but his final proof testimony claimed that he actually established his residence there in 1901. The same document says that he was born in El Rito, New Mexico in 1845, three years before American sovereignty. The ruins of his three room house and barn are still faintly visible on the land. His property was sold to Jose Angél Cisneros in 1921. His daughter, Juanita, was the mother of our friend, Baudelio Garcia. She and her husband Antonio would later own the property before selling it to other Anglo part timers in the 1950s.

Albino Duran's neighbor to the east was Felix Martinez who acquired his 53 acres in 1919. He had been a witness for Albino Duran in 1916 and said he lived about a mile away from Duran, so once again, it seems likely that his actual residency substantially pre existed the patent date. Census records show him still living in the valley in 1930 when he was seventy five years old.

The last successful Santa Rita homesteader was Emilio Martinez whose patent for sixty nine acres was dated December 13, 1927, during the administration of Calvin Coolidge. Martinez took up a lapsed claim that had been initiated in 1909 by Feliz Lopez and subsequently taken over by Carlos Jaramillo. A 1914 homestead entry survey contains language reflecting the difficulties faced by even these last settlers in the valley. The surveyor reported: "Improvements made upon and for the benefit of this claim by original applicant, Felix Lopez, and now held by Carlos Jaramillo, are in poor condition ... Log and adobe dwelling house, 14 x 30 ft. ... house is not habitable ...but could be repaired. Val. $100. ...Adobe house; 20 x 40 ft. ... only partially completed. $25."

The same report graphically described the neighborhood.

Ortiz, Colorado, the nearest post office, is about 20 miles east over poor wagon road. Toltec, the nearest railroad point is approximately two miles to the N. and can be reached by a good trail. Antonito, Colorado, a railroad center and town of approximately 2,500 is 26 miles to the east. San Miguel, a small native settlement, is 8 miles to the east," (Survey completed Sept. 8, 1914)

The Martinez patent marked the end of the Santa Rita version of the centuries long march to the north in the persistent quest of the Hispano people to expand their homeland. The journey was completed in the upper reaches of one of the myriad small rivers and streams that were the magnets for their migration. Within a few short decades most of the settlers would be gone from the valley, off in pursuit of a new kind of dream. They were replaced by a new brand of people, most of them from the emerging majority culture. They were part timers. They didn't come to make a living. They came to enjoy living. Some of the old people drifted out of Santa Rita but their descendants were still out there, some of them in the lower, more hospitable parts of the greater San Luis Valley and others in the greater beyond. Like the descendants of other Hispano village people, many still remember Santa Rita as their homeland. And in Santa Rita, those who remained continued the old ways for a time before they too moved on into the new American mainstream.

The Old And The New

THE FIRST HALF OF THE TWENTIETH CENTURY in Santa Rita was marked both by continuity and change. There was continuity in the persistence of the old way of life that in many ways was little different from that experienced by people of earlier generations. But there was also the beginning of dramatic change in the cultural and political environment that would soon bring an end to the old ways.

The movement of settlers into the canyon followed the old pattern of contiguous expansion observed in the period before 1800. That is, people moved out from the downstream villages like Ortiz, Los Pinos and San Miguel to start the new upstream community. The homestead files often listed Ortiz, Colorado as the Post Office address of homesteaders and their witnesses. The village of Ortiz was a thriving community with a population of about five hundred people in 1900. The church next to the Post Office was dedicated to San Juan Nepomuceno, the patron Saint of irrigation, testifying to the continued central role of acequias in the Rio de Los Pinos valley.

The record of upstream settlement described in the previous chapter shows that the homesteaders established residency over a period of about two decades, from 1888 to 1910. The patent dates ranged between 1911 and 1919, except for two outliers in 1927.

As was noted earlier, many settlers seemed to have moved onto the lands well before they proved up their claims. Perhaps they were obliged to wait for the establishment of the Carson National Forest in 1908 before pursuing their applications. In any event, the settlement of Santa Rita was completed during the last decade of the nineteenth century and the first decade of the twentieth century.

What happened during those years appears to have mirrored the pattern of many earlier settlements in the long history of the Hispano march north. It probably started with the challenge of building a rough wagon road into the canyon, a burden probably carried by the earliest claimants such as Jose Basilio Duran and Albino Duran. We can only speculate on the details.

The work involved in building houses, corrals, barns and fences must have been daunting and probably called on help from extended families and neighbors. We know that the massive job of building acequias and diversion dams would have been a communal effort as it had been throughout the history of New Mexico. The land also had to be cleared and prepared for home construction and irrigation. And as it was described in the Taos County example, the work of acequia building had to be done by the people with primitive tools and equipment and the limited help of work animals. Every final proof affidavit signed by the homesteaders described their efforts to cultivate and irrigate their land to produce a variety of crops. Most of what they produced was used to support their subsistence life style but the records show that some crops were sold for cash.

Cash was a relatively new concept for the settlers. The Anglo new comers came in huge numbers after the civil war and the arrival of the railroad in the 1880s brought more people, money and new ways. The railroad revolutionized the region, bringing people and, more importantly, businesses that drew some young men out of the family based agricultural economy. Also, by the 1880s, a new kind of large scale, capital intensive irrigated agriculture created a need for wage labor. By this time hundreds of thousands of new acres had been brought under cultivation and massive irrigation canals had been built in the San Luis Valley. The Anglo farmers and business men were becoming the dominant culture in the Valley.

Nevertheless, at the remote edges of this new world, life went on much as it had for centuries. Others have reported on the persistence of tradition in southern Colorado and northern New Mexico. And conversations with older people who have memories of living in Santa Rita or remember stories told to them as children, prove that the old ways were very much alive in early twentieth century Santa Rita.

Housekeeping was hard work and required the help of everyone in the family. There was no electricity or indoor plumbing. One can only imagine what it was like to do the laundry, especially in the winter. Water came from the river or the acequia and the children spent considerable time carrying it up to the house. Cooking was done on wood stoves that also provided heat for the house. Cutting, collecting, splitting and storing fire wood, leña, was part of everyday life.

During the long cold winters the men cut ice from the river and stored it with saw dust in outside cellars where it would usually last through the summer and into the next winter. Children learned that they should never open the cellar door without Mother's permission.

One witness recalls that in the 1930s and 1940s, his mother would go to town to shop perhaps once or twice a month. She walked up to the train track, flagged down the train and rode into Antonito. When she started her trip the children accompanied her up the trail to the train, pulling a homemade wagon that would be used to carry the supplies back to the cabin when she returned on a later train. Food was simple but satisfying. They ate a lot of beans, chile and tortillas. They grew their own potatoes—sometimes they were purple—which were surprisingly successful at this high altitude with its short growing season. His mother had a kitchen garden that produced other vegetables during the short summer. They also harvested meat from their cattle, sheep and pigs. There were no surviving elk in the area at that time since they had become extinct in New Mexico as a result of over hunting, but there were deer and with the help of salt licks, they enjoyed venison occasionally on a year round basis.

Life was risky. Accidents were inevitable and when disease struck there was little medical help to be had. In the event of serious illness, the only option was a long wagon or train trip to Antonito to see a doctor if one was available and could be afforded. They had their own folk remedies, using local plants and herbs, and there were people they turned to for their special skills. One of my reporters said, "Papa Joe Sisneros was a Curandero." Another recalled his mother and others suffering from a form of sleeping sickness that they called pesaría. He remembers, "I thought she was going to die."

Deaths and births were challenging events in the wilderness. As death approached, there was little the family could do beyond praying and providing comfort and support. When the ordeal was over, the family prepared the body, built a rough casket and conducted the burial, usually in the family camposanto (cemetery) or perhaps in a larger cemetery in San Miguel or Ortiz. The people were all devoted Catholics and would have preferred to have a priest officiate at the funeral, but priests were few and far between. The lay brotherhood of Penitentes was very active in the larger neighborhood and sometimes the family asked for their assistance in formalizing the event. The Penitentes and the family were able to solemnize the service by singing alabadas, traditional hymns. It was also customary to have wakes (velorios) in honor of the deceased. The family served refreshments to the guests and music, particularly singing, could be a part of the ceremomy.

The families were large and there were many births in the valley. Sometimes the mothers were able to anticipate the event and take the long wagon trip to Ortiz or Antonito where they could have more professional help. Doctors were seldom available but the services of a midwife (partera) were often provided. Occasionally the family could bring the partera to Santa Rita, but more often than not the baby was born with only the help of neighbors or the women in the family.

Weddings were frequently conducted in the churches in San Miguel or Ortiz and could usually be performed by a priest. There were several circuit riding priests in the region who served the many little churches and capillas scattered among the many small villages in that part of Colorado and New Mexico. It was common for the bride's family to have a party, called a prendorio, to celebrate the event. A locally produced moonshine often was served. I am told that stills were operated at the sites of mountain springs in the area.

Music and dancing were a big part of social life. At Christmas and New Years there were plays and pageants, some in the new Anglo mode and others that came from historical Spanish tradition. Children and adults went house to house, singing and enjoying food and drink, a practice called Miscrismas in this neighborhood. My older friends from the valley recall that there was frequently an old man in ragged clothing, who wandered around frightening the children. He may have been a character out of the Christmas

Eve tradition of the aguello or abuelo (grandfather), usually an old man in a mask, who went to homes to see if the children were being good.

There was a lively social life in the larger area that included the downstream villages. Many people played musical instruments including fiddles, accordions, banjos and, of course, guitars, and everyone knew many songs. There were dance halls in the larger villages such as Ortiz and Los Pinos. The dances and parties and the associated alcoholic beverages were an important source of entertainment and, not surprisingly, occasional aggression and violence. That combination undoubtedly contributed to the following story:

> On a recent drive down the canyon with two of my older witnesses of the old days, one of them suddenly pointed to a tall old ponderosa pine and said, "Do you see that tree? That's where Maximo shot that guy!" He said that the victim had met one of Maximo's daughters at a dance hall down in Los Pinos. It seems that he "fell in love with her" and started to hang around her father's house where he was not welcome. So Maximo shot him. I asked if the man was killed and he said, "No." They took him up to the train and they got him to the hospital in Alamosa, and then he died. When asked if Maximo got in trouble because of the shooting and the man's death, he said, "Oh, no. The guy was a trespasser and Maximo didn't want him as a son in law!" Maybe it helped that Maximo was a famous game warden and therefore the closest thing to "the law" in that part of the territory!

That story and others were told on a drive up and down the Santa Rita Canyon on a crisp fall day when I was accompanied by two men who had lived in the canyon with their families during the days we have been discussing. As we moved along at a leisurely pace, every hundred yards of our slow drive brought forth a remembered name or story. Every distant vista triggered a memory: "I herded my family's sheep herd up there." Perhaps some of the memories were rose colored: "This stream used to run all summer" or "The snow used to be much deeper than it is now." But the place was alive with recollection. "Mama used to say, we don't live in Santa Rita; we live in Los Crestones."

Every side canyon had a name. Every old house or place where there had been a house had a named family. The two old school houses, still standing, had remembered teachers' names and stories about school days. The two schools were part of the Rio Arriba County School System. I asked, "Was the instruction in both Spanish and English?" The answer, "No, only in English!" The teaching, the texts and materials were all in English despite the fact the teacher spoke Spanish and the children spoke no English.

One day the children saw an Anglo fisherman (i.e., an outsider) in the river. My friend thinks they called him a bolío, the word they thought was Spanish for "fisherman." When they asked the teacher what was the English word for bolío, he told them it was "rolling pin."

School was a luxury that could not be consistently enjoyed by the children of that day. One of my riding historians said that even in the second or third grade, his father took him out of school to help with the family sheep or other chores. The two little one room school houses in Santa Rita and similar schools down river in San Miguel, Los Pinos and Ortiz could provide, at best, only a bare minimum elementary program. To go beyond those early grades was almost impossible for most people.

The closest high school was almost twenty miles and many hours away for most students. Despite that, many people found a way. Some, like Baudelio Garcia's parents, managed to send their children to distant boarding schools, such as the Protestant Church supported McCurdy School in Santa Cruz, near Española. McCurdy provided a boarding school experience for many rural Hispano students who had limited educational opportunities at home. At one period in his youth, Baudelio and other students were sent by their parents to live in Sanford, Colorado, during the winter school year so that they could attend public high school there.

In our drive up the canyon we passed cabins built by the homesteaders and now used as part time getaways by the new, mostly Anglo owners. My friends remembered the many other houses that used to be there. They remembered that in addition to the more permanent houses, there were many small shacks or huts that were use temporarily or seasonally by the settlers or others. They called them as huertas mexicanas. The conventional Spanish for such structures would be cabañas or chozos. I was also told that people who had their residence on the south side of the river, had huertas mexicanas on the north side that they used as temporary quarters when the heavy spring runoff prevented them from safely crossing the river to their homes.

During our canyon drive, one person's memory stimulated a reaction from the other. They shifted reflexively from English to Spanish and took up the thread of common recall, remembering people, place names and events they thought they had forgotten. One remembered the old mailman who came up to fish in the river and brought with him their mail; mail they would otherwise not have received until they made the long trip to the post office in Ortiz. One remembered a special trip he had taken as a child. He and his mother had climbed up to Toltec and boarded the train that took them all the way to Durango and back, a memorable journey.

The other recalled the day when he and his wife heard an unexpected knock on their door one early morning. It was a hobo who dropped off the train up above and came down into the valley expecting who knows what. They kept him employed and fed for a week or so before he climbed back up the mountain to the train and resumed his journey.

The role of the Penitentes has been mentioned several times. The people of the valley with memories of mid twentieth century life along the Rio de Los Pinos and in the neighboring villages in Colorado, say that the Penitentes played a big role there. A 1909 survey map of the village of San Miguel, shows the location of the Catholic Church and another building identified as the "Penitente Church" which would more properly be called the Morada. The lovely old stone church is still there but the morada has long since disappeared. There were also moradas in Los Pinos, Ortiz, San Antonio and many other locations in Conejos County and throughout the Upper Rio Grande region.

Jasper Lopez, who told me some of the stories repeated here, was born in 1931 and lived with his parents and brothers and sisters on the homestead originally patented to Feliz Martinez. He knew many men who were members of the Penitente Brothehood. He said that as a young man he had wanted to join the organization, "but my Mother wouldn't let me," a testament to the power and influence of Hispano mothers.

Jasper remembered the Holy Week observances of the Brotherhood that included public penance and some form of flagellation. He says it was the practice for the men to cut their backs with sharp pieces of glass that had been heated over a flame to prevent infection. He also recalls the processions that included a man carrying the large cross up a nearby hill (the Calvario).

The Penitente Brotherhood, more formally known as El Hermanidad de Nuestro Padre Jesús Nazareno, is a lay Catholic organization that traces its roots to medieval Spain. There is significant scholarly disagreement regarding the path of the organization to New Mexico, but its historical presence is not disputed. It was originally called La Santa Hermanidad de La Sangre de Nuestra Señor Jesucristo. New Mexico's famous Bishop and later Archbishop Lamy sought to tame what he saw as the excesses of this wild, frontier Hispano phenomenon. He was particularly concerned with the practice of flagellation and the symbolism portrayed by the reference to "the blood of Christ." Those concerns caused him to outlaw the organization for a time. But after mandating changes, he relented. In 1880, as a result of Bishop Lamy's efforts the group became known as La Confradía de Nuestro Padre Jesús Nazareno. So in the end the church devised an acceptable role for the Penitentes.

However, the people at the remote edge of the Archdiocese persisted in some of the unauthorized practices long after they had been officially banned. While the Penitentes are most famous or notorious in the Anglo world for the practice of flagellation, they had many positive roles to play. They were a mutual aid institution in the Hispano community, performed much needed charitable acts during times of need and helped sustain the religious and cultural life of the people.

Our focus here has been on the continuity of the old ways that displayed amazing resiliency even into the middle of the twentieth century. But the few survivors of that time and their children are the last witnesses to the final days of the cohesive pioneer community in Santa Rita canyon. That community persisted longer than many of its sister villages further south in New Mexico, where the process of depopulation began a bit earlier. Richard Nostrand described 1900 as the heyday of the Hispano Homeland, a time when it included parts of the five states of New Mexico, Colorado, Texas, Oklahoma and Arizona.

It will be recalled that the census district covering the area from the state line to Los Crestones was called Precinct 15. In that district the population seems to have peaked in 1910 when the population was about 735. The 1920 census listed 320 people and in 1930, that number declined to 122. An incident in 1931 suggests that the 1930 number may have been and under count. It also shows that the new Americans were learning how to use the tools of politics. The office of the Postmaster General announced that the Ortiz post office would be closed. The people affected were outraged and filed a petition protesting the closure. The petition stated in part that:

> ... more than 225 persons receive their mail at said post office, that more than 150 of the patrons live in New Mexico, ... that many of the patrons ... do not come to Ortiz oftener than once a week, on account of the distance and the bad roads. That the rural carrier cannot possibly deliver mail to boxes within any reasonable distance of the homes of many of the patrons, especially the following named settlements, viz: Santa Rita, fifteen miles from Ortiz; San Antonio Creek, twelve miles from Ortiz; San Miguel, 8 miles from Ortiz; Toltec, some 16 miles from Ortiz; Sublet, some 12 miles from Ortiz; and Big Horn, some 8 miles from Ortiz.

The petition was signed by 238 people from both states and only two of the signers had Anglo names. Copies of the petition were mailed to New Mexico's Governor Arthur Seligman, Senators Bronson Cutting and Sam Bratton and to then Congressman Dennis Chaves. Governor Seligman responded cordially to the petitioners and assured them he would do "everything possible" to keep the post office open. Those efforts apparently bore fruit because the post office remained open for most of that decade and the derelict old building still stands today.

In Santa Rita, the population numbers continued to be fairly robust. In 1920, the census reported about 47 people in about 11 families. In 1930, there were about 47 people in 12 families, including perhaps four of the original homesteaders. In the following decade and even more so in the 1940s, the population decline was precipitous. The surviving households tended to be headed by older people and more of the young men were leaving for what they saw as greener pastures. This phenomenon was prevalent throughout the homeland. People were abandoning the traditional agricultural life and moving to the urban, capital driven and increasingly Anglo dominated world. The 1940s and the Second World War brought dramatic change to all of rural America, and the Hispano Homeland was no exception.

Surely there was much to admire in the strength, courage and independence required to carve out a livelihood in a harsh environment. But subsistence farming is usually chosen as a life style only when there are few options. In the 1940 there began to be options and even if the perceived benefits were sometimes illusory, the options were taken; jobs, towns, cities, schools, medical care, the cash economy, a chance for a better life.

The history of North America is inextricably linked to the waves of immigrants that came to the new world beginning in the seventeenth century and continuing even today. And the newcomers were often feared and resented by those who were already here. In that respect, the experience of the Hispano people was truly unique. Unlike any other early Americans, they lived for two and a half centuries in a homogeneous culture of their own making, unchallenged by any significant European arrivals. They were isolated even from their own Spanish and Mexican roots. There was little dilution of their cultural and ethnic DNA. There was very little in migration during that long period, not even from Mexico. The first American census in 1850, showed that the total population of New Mexico included only 370 people identified as "Mexican." By contrast, the early eastern Americans were subject to a never ending series of new arrivals representing differ- ent national origins, languages, religions and cultures. Contrastingly, the

Hispano community had been dominant and uncontested in its homeland until the arrival of "The Americans."

Suddenly the historic residents became a part of a new country within which they were treated as foreigners and became a minority group in their ancient homeland. The Americans displaced their historic hegemony and arrived with a disparaging view of the "Mexicans," whom they had recently defeated in the Mexican War. The natives, as they came to be called, still lived in their virtually one hundred percent Hispano communities, but the communities became isolated islands in an overwhelming Anglo sea.

Spanish continued to be the language off their families and villages but they had become Americans. They generally embraced their new citizenship but there were challenges. In Santa Rita they still lived on their Hispano Island but they were increasingly affected by the Anglo mainland. They paid property taxes to Rio Arriba County. Their children were exposed to the English language in the county schools. They borrowed money and mortgaged their property to Anglo lenders. Family members were employed, usually part time, by the railroad, the Forest Service, Conejos and Rio Arriba County and by Mormon farmers. They earned dollars that they spent in Anglo mercantile establishments. And as time passed, they began to sell their homesteads to Anglo outsiders who found new values in the properties in the high country wilderness.

In Santa Rita, that process started in the mid 1940s, and by ten years later, most of the upper canyon lands had passed into the hands of Anglo purchasers from Santa Fe, Las Cruces and even Pawhuska, Oklahoma. Among the new landowner names were Richard (Moon) Mullins, William Lynn, David Carmody, G. C. Lassiter, Pete Irwin, T. B. White, Albert Clancy, Charlie White, Clay Hudson and Donald Stuart. Baudelio and Arlene Garcia and his parents Antonio and Juanita Garcia were left as the only survivors of the homestead family generations. The Garcias remained in the valley, maintaining the acequias and diversion dams, irrigating the meadows, cutting and baling hay, grazing their animals and providing expertise and much needed support to the less skilled newcomers.

As this chronology suggests, there was a period in the 1940s and 1950s when Santa Rita was in transition from exclusively Hispano to majority Anglo ownership. Some of the Hispanos lived part time in Santa Rita and part time in San Miguel or some more distant place while still working the land as the newcomers were establishing their seasonal use of the properties. One of Baudelio Garcia's nephews is Chris Garcia, who now owns the senior Garcia's old Adobe cabin. As a child, he lived part time in Santa Rita with his family. His father, Baudelio's brother was a teacher, and worked mostly in the Rio Arriba County system. Another brother was also a teacher who worked in the Conejos County schools. These two brothers exemplify the family commitment to the importance of education. A further example of that commitment is Chris Garcia, who not only graduated from college but went on to the University of New Mexico School of law and is now a practicing attorney in Albuquerque. He and his siblings were the first in the family for whom English is the first language and Chris admits he to struggles to speak Spanish comfortably.

Despite these exceptions from the rule and the increased presence of the new Anglo influence in the valley, Spanish was still the first language of the people there, and sometimes there was confusion and misunderstanding by the new neighbors on both sides of the language divide. Chris Garcia remembers that his mother had difficulty accurately pronouncing the unfamiliar Anglo names of Mr. Mullins and Mr. Carmody. He said she called them Melones and Carmota. Some of the young men from the neighborhood improved their English language skills while serving in the military during the Second World War and the Korean conflict. Chris Garcia's father joined the Army during the Korean War.

As the people began to give up their small irrigated homesteads in Santa Rita and dozens of other villages across northern New Mexico, they often moved to the larger towns and cities in the region. In most cases, unlike in Santa Rita, there were no ready buyers for the old properties and many people maintained ownership or transferred their property to other family members. Even when they moved great distances away, often to Arizona or California, as many did, they maintained a strong bond with their place or village of origin. As indicated in my interview with Jasper Lopez and Baudelio

Garcia, the Hispano people identify intensely with their home country and recall vividly the details of its landscape. This connection to what Nostrand calls their "patria chica" is intensely alive among the descendants of the Rio de Los Pinos settlers. In the second decade of the twenty first century, there are still regular reunions in the village of San Miguel, attended by families from all over the southwest. Some of them represent families whose ancestors left the land as much as a hundred years before.

Whether they were called "Americanos" or Anglos, their arrival changed the social and political status of the Hispanos significantly. They became citizens and some would say second class citizens at the same time. The differing values and life experiences of the two peoples made conflict and discrimination inevitable, and the Anglo newcomers soon had the upper hand. Most of the Americans believed: "that they represented a superior civilization, and with contempt they described New Mexicans as indolent, degenerate, undependable, dishonest, impoverished, and addicted to gambling and other vices .... Not surprisingly, the attitude of the Hispanos was equally unfavorable: "Americanos, as all were called, were thought to be arrogant, rude, insolent, economic materialists, religious heretics, and cultural barbarians." (Nostrand)

So these were the perspectives of some of the people who came together in the towns and cities to which the Hispanos were migrating in the 1940s and 1950s. The resiliency and adaptability that had helped them survive in the past served them well in the new environment. As they had in the villages, they banded together in the towns to meet the challenges of discrimination.

Some of those challenges were served by a new organization formed in Antonito in 1900. It was called La Sociedad Protección Mutuo de Trabajadores Unidos, perhaps better known by its initials SPMDTU or simply La Sociedad. It was one of many Hispanic self help organizations that sprang up in the late 1800s and early 1900s. Its goal was to provide mutual aid to its members and the community. The SPMDTU grew rapidly and came to have sixty five local chapters or "concilios" in southern Colorado, northern New Mexico and Utah. There were concilios in Ortiz, Los Pinos and San Muguel, some of whose members were Santa Rita homesteaders. La Sociedad was one of the early civil rights organizations created to protect Hispano land rights, language and culture. It also provided low cost insurance, financial aid to the families of the Hermanos and helped its members fight against wage discrimination.

Probably the most painful injury suffered by the Hispanos at the hand of the Anglo intruders was the damage done to their property rights. We have briefly described the fate of the Spanish and Mexican community land grants. These grants gave small tracts to individual families and required the community to construct acequias and do what was necessary to cultivate and irrigate their farms. But just as important, the grants also provided often vast tracts of land to be used on common by the settlers for grazing, timber harvesting and fire wood gathering. These common lands, the ejidos, were essential to the survival of the community and were to be held in common in perpetuity.

The concept of a community ownership interest in real estate was completely foreign to the Americans and conflicted with their concept of individual ownership rights. The wholesale ignorance of Spanish and Mexican law and tradition, plus the unbridled hunger of the new people from the east for land, water and resources, deprived the local people of their rights which were to be honored under the Treaty of Guadalupe Hidalgo. The Conejos Grant of over 2.5 million acres was totally rejected by the Court of Private Claims in 1900, primarily on the basis that the original grant documents couldn't be produced. The Sange de Cristo Grant was approved in mid century by the Surveyor General but was later sold by Carlos Beaubien and his partners to large corporate interests, which deprived the Hispano landowners of access to the ejido. They received deeds to their small residential and farming tracts but lost the timber and grazing rights they had when Beaubien owned the land.

Despite their cultural, language, economic and legal disadvantages, many of Hispanic people adapted effectively to life in the new Anglo environment. One area where they excelled was politics. It was more difficult in Colorado where they had become a distinct minority on a state wide basis, but New Mexico was another story. During territorial days, Hispanos were a strong majority, especially in the north. Between 1850 and 1912, twelve of the eighteen Delegates to the United States House of Representatives were Hispanos. Of that number, six were Democrats and six were Republicans. After statehood, only eight of the 32 individuals who have served have been Hispanos, but three of them, Antonio Fernandez, Manuel Lujan and Bill Richardson served many terms in that office. Of course Bill Richardson was not a New Mexico Hispano, but it would have been hard to tell the difference at one of his town hall meetings.

Since 1912, sixteen men have served New Mexico in the Senate. Three of them have been Hispanos, but two of them were in office for very long periods; Dennis Chavez from 1935 until 1960 and Joseph Montoya from 1965 until 1877. Those statistics, however, don't tell the story of Hispano political dominance in the heart of their homeland, north central New Mexico. In several northern counties, they maintained their population advantage for many decades and it was reflected in their political success.

Rio Arriba is a case in point. It has often been said that politics was the main industry in the county, and that's not far from the truth as county, school and forest service jobs plus the other patronage positions that came along with "The New Deal" provided the lion's share of employment opportunities in Rio Arriba. In territorial and early statehood days the county was solid Republican country. Benigno C. Hernandez was regularly elected to county offices and, in 1914, was the first Hispano to be elected to the Congress after statehood. He was a Republican.

The great depression, Franklin Delano Roosevelt and The New Deal changed all that. The Democratic Party and its powerful public works stimulus suddenly brought about a change of heart among the pragmatic politicians of Rio Arriba County. It became a Democratic stronghold over night By mid century a strong new leader emerged in the person of the famous Emilio Naranjo, who became the undisputed political boss. He served as a state senator and was the Rio Arriba County Democratic Chairman for almost forty years. His was universally credited with building the most effective and lasting political machine in the state. The mythology of Naranjo and Democratic control in the north is epitomized by an often told apocryphal story about an election during the long tenure of Senator Dennis Chavez. A Chavez official at party headquarters on election night was reported to have called a voting place in Rio Arriba county and asked, "How many votes for Chavez?" The answer was, "How many do you need?"

We don't find much evidence for what politics were like in the far northern territory of Rio Arriba Precinct 15, but it would probably be an interesting tale. Across the line in Colorado it was a different story. The Hispano politicians had considerable success at the local level but they were a small minority in state wide races. During the territorial period and for the first hundred years and more of statehood, no Hispano was elected to either house of Congress. It was not until 2004 that Ken Salazar was elected as the first Hispano from Colorado in the Senate. His brother, John Salazar was elected to the House of Representatives in the same year to represent the sprawling district that includes the San Luis Valley. After serving in the Senate, Ken Salazar was named as Secretary of the Interior by President Obama.

The Salazar story is in some ways typical of those told by many Hispanics whose families followed the little rivers north to Colorado. The Salazars apparently came to New Mexico sometime in the 1600s, and by the early 1800s, Ken Salazar's great- great- great grandfather lived in Chamita, which it will be recalled was briefly the Rio Arriba county seat. A son of that ancestor came to Colorado's San Luis Valley in the mid 1800s. The family still farms and ranches the same land at Los Rincones, near the junction of the Conejos River and Rio San Antonio.

By the time Ken Salazar and his brother John were elected to the Congress, it was no longer an unusual accomplishment. The Congressional Hispanic Caucus comprises twenty one Democratic members at this writing and the Republican alternative, the Congressional Hispanic Conference has ten members. Hispanics or Latinos represent 16% of the population and most of them are from cultures and national origins other than the New Mexico based Hispano community that has been the subject of this book. There are now dozens of hyphenated Americans, including Cuban-

Americans, Dominican-Americans and Mexican-Americans that comprise the country's Hispano population. While we have highlighted their role in politics, members of this hugely diverse category of people have achieved success in virtually every field of human endeavor. The same can be said for the small sub group we have called Hispanos. They take their place as a minority within a minority as defined by contemporary demographic classification. However, even as they have merged into the American mainstream, they continue to proudly preserve their cultural customs, beliefs, values and language. By doing so, they make a lasting contribution to the rich diversity of the country.

Conclusion

THIS BRINGS US NOT TO THE END of the story but to the end of this telling of the story. The Santa Rita Canyon in far northern New Mexico where much of this story took place has evolved throughout geologic time and will continue to change in the future. Over time, very different people have lived in and used the place and that kind of change will also continue. But with effort and care, the things that have been valued here including its history and its beauty, will continue to be honored.

This tale began with the arrival in this hemisphere of the ancestors of the hardy souls who followed the rivers north to this narrow canyon on the Rio de Los Pinos. This small neighborhood in the mountains was the ultimate destination of a handful of people who were part of a four century long trek north to draw the final northern boundary of The Hispano Homeland. They brought with them a unique subculture of Spanish civilization, spoke the language of Cervantes and lived to put their imprint on the land, the rivers and the communities they created here.

Drawing on their medieval Spanish roots, they were village dwellers and expanded their frontier by creating small communities along the dozens of tributary streams of the Rio Grande, the mother river. They lived among and often in conflict with the native people who were here long before they arrived. A small sample of those people chose Santa Rita Canyon, mostly because it was the last best place available where they could hope to make a living. With time it became their patria chica, and they cherished it as their home within the homeland.

It was a remote and difficult place but for a while they lived there relatively undisturbed and insulated from the Anglo onslaught from the new country in the east. Finally they began to move on to find their place in that new country, learning how to succeed in a different culture with a new language while trying to preserve what they treasured most in the old world. The monuments to their time here are nontraditional. There are the many villages, though they are much diminished. There are hundreds of small churches, many of them lovingly preserved and restored as symbols of the communities they served. There are countless distinctive camposantos, many with hand crafted grave markers.

Hand crafter grave markers, Max Quintana, San Miguel Cemetery; Francisco Archuleta, Santa Rita Camposanto

In some villages, long abandoned rustic houses are slowly returning to the earth. The strongest reminders of the past and the most convincing evidence of sustainability are the hundreds of surviving acequias and diversion dams that still take the water from the little rivers that brought the people north.

Rio de Los Pinos Acequia.

We take a final look at Santa Rita Canyon as it is today. The original twelve homesteads now comprise properties spread out over the five mile long canyon, now owned mostly by people who came from outside the neighborhood. Only three of the owners are Hispanos. The first is our friend Baudelio Garcia and his wife Arlene. He is the grandson of two homesteaders.

Baudelio's mother, father, Arlene and Baudelio Garcia.

The second is Chris Garcia, the great grandson of the same two homesteaders. He represents the strong gravitational pull to return to the patria chica, having purchased the old place where his grandparents lived. The third Hispano owners are a husband and wife who started their lives in El Rito and Española, migrated to California to make a living and returned to northern New Mexico, as so many do, after they retired.

The rest of us came here from different roots to find peace, beauty and comfort in an environment that had been an existential challenge to the original homesteaders. Knowing something of Santa Rita's history, one has to be torn between thinking of the place as it was and as it is. It was a community, however transient and fragile, carved out of the wilderness and given the ambitious name "Santa Rita Township." It is today a place of great beauty and cultural value, drawing on both its environmental attributes and the remnant reminders of its history.

It properly belongs to all who value it out of their different heritages. Perhaps Baudelio Garcia and I see it through a different lens but when we sit together at sunset, listen to the river, watch the birds and look for the elk and coyotes, we share something that comes to each of us from the place. We know it will change in the future as it has in the past but think it should persist as a special place that should be enjoyed, protected and preserved by all who come after us.

Bibliography

All Trails Lead to Santa Fe: An Anthology Commemorating the 400th Anniversary of the Founding of Santa Fe, New Mexico, in 1610. Santa Fe: Sunstone Press, 2010.

Bailey, L. Robinson. *Indian Slave Trade in the Southwest.* Los Angeles: Westernlore Press, 1966.

Brooks, James F. *Captives and Cousins.* Chapel Hill and London: University of North Carolina, 2002.

Baxter, John O. "Spanish Irrigation in the Taos Valley." Office of the State Engineer. Santa Fe, New Mexico, 1990.

Baxter, John O. Las Carnerados: *Sheep Trade in New Mexico 1700–1860.* Albuquerque: University of New Mexico Press, 1987.

Carlson, Alvar W. *The Spanish American Homeland: Four Centuries in New Mexico's Rio Arriba County.* Baltimore: John Hopkins University Press, 1990.

Carr, Matthew. *Blood and Faith. The Purging of Muslim Spain.* New York: The New Press, 2009.

Chavez, Fray Angelico. *My Penetente Land: Reflections on Spanish New Mexico.* New Edition, Santa Fe: Sunstone Press, 2012.

Cobos, Rubén. *A Dictionary of New Mexico and Southern Colorado Spanish.* Santa Fe: Museum of New Mexico Press, 2003.

Colville, Ruth Marie. *La Vereda, A Trail Through Time.* Alamosa, Colorado: The San Luis Valley Historical Society, 1996.

Dean, Rob, ed. *Santa Fe, Its 400th Year: Exploring the Past, Defining the Future.* Santa Fe: Sunstone Press, 2010.

Dunlay, Tom. *Kit Carson and the Indians.* Lincoln and London: University of Nebraska Press, 2000

Ebright, Malcolm. "Genízaros." New Mexico Office of the State Historian. The New Mexico State Records Center and Archives, 2004–2010. www. newmexicohistory.org

Espinosa, Aurelio M. *The Folklore of Spain in the American Southwest*, Norman: University of Oklahoma Press, 1976

Cheetham, Francis. "Early Settlements of Southern Colorado." *Colorado Magazine*, Vol. 5, No. 1, 1928

Groom, Winston. *Kearney's March*. New York: Alfred A. Knopf, 2011

Gwynne, S.C. *Empire of the Summer Moon*. New York: Scribner, 2010

Hordes, Stanley M. *To The End of the Earth: A History of the Crypto Jews of New Mexico*. New York: Columbia University Press, 2008

Hurt, R. Douglas. *The Indian Frontier, 1763–1846*. Albuquerque: University of New Mexico Press, 2002

Kamen, Henry. *The Disinherited. Exile and the Making of Spanish Culture*. New York: Harper Collins, 2007

Lopez-Tushar, Olibama. *The People of El Valle*. Third Edition. Pueblo: El Escritorio, 1997

Lovato, Andrew Leo. *Santa Fe Hispanic Culture*. Albuquerque: University of New Mexico Press, 2004

May, Esther V. Cordova. *Antes: Stories From The Past, Rural Cuba, New Mexico, 1769–1949*. Santa Fe: Sunstone Press, 2011

McCourt, Purnee A. "The Conejos Land Grant of Southern Colorado." *Colorado Magazine*, LII/ 1, 1975

Meacham, Jon. *American Lion*. New York: Random House, 2008

Mead, Frances Harvey. *Conejos County*. Colorado Springs: Century One Press, 1984

Merry, Robert W. *A Country of Vast Designs*. New York: Simon and Shuster, 2009

Montaño, Mary. *Tradiciones Nuevomexicanas*. Albuquerque: University of New Mexico Press, 2001

Nostrand, Richard L. *The Hispano Homeland*. Norman: University of Oklahoma Press, 1992.

Osterwald, Doris B. *Ticket to Toltec*. Lakewood, Colorado: Western Guideways, 1980.

Padget, Martin. *Indian Country Travels in the American Southwest, 1840–1935*. Albuquerque: University of New Mexico Press, 2004.

Parkhill, Forbes. "Colorado's First Survey." *Colorado Magazine*, 33, July, 1956.

Phillips, Fred M., Hall, G. Emlen & Black, Mary E. *Reining In the Rio Grande.* Albuquerque: University of New Mexico Press, 2011.

Remley, David. *Kit Carson. The Life of an American Border Man.* Norman: University of Oklahoma Press, 2011.

Rivera José A. La Sociedad. *Guardians of Hispanic Culture Along the Rio Grande.* Albuquerque: University of New Mexico Press, 2010.

Salazar de Valdez, Olivama & Valdez de Pong, Dolores. *Life in Los Sauces.* Monte Vista, Colorado: Adobe Village Press, 2005.

Spencer, Frank C. *The Story of the San Luis Valley.* Alamosa, Colorado: The San Luis Valley Historical Society, 1975.

Torrez, Robert J. & Trapp, Robert. Rio Arriba. *A New Mexico County.* Los Ranchos, New Mexico: Rio Grande Books, 2010.

Velasquez, Melitón. "Guadalupe Colony Was Founded 1854." *Colorado Magazine*, 34, 1957.

West, Elizabeth, ed. *Santa Fe: 400 Years, 400 Questions.* Santa Fe: Sunstone Press, 2012

Woodworth, Stephen E. *Manifest Destinies.* New York: Random House, 2011.

Wroth, William H. "Pueblo de Abiquiu, A Genízaro Community." New Mexico Office of the State Historian. New Mexico State Record Center and Archives, 2004–2010.

Other Resources

Interviews

Rose Garcia Trujillo: September 30, 1998
Baudelio and Arlene Garcia: Early 2000s
Chris Garcia: October 6, 2010
Chris Garcia and Paul Stewart: October 7, 2010
Baudelio Garcia: October 8, 2010
Amarante and Frances Martinez: July 21, 2011
Jaspar Lopez and Baudelio Garcia: October 11, 2011

Land Title Records. Department of the Interior, Bureau of Land Management, Record of Homestead Patents , www.glorecords.blm.gov (current as of May 2012)

Census Records for Taos and Rio Arriba Counties for years 1850, 1860, 1870, 1880, 1900, 1910, 1920 and 1930; Microfilm records at New Mexico State Record Center and Archives, Santa Fe, New Mexico.

Newspaper articles, *Santa Fe New Mexican.* January 10, 2009 (Tom Sharpe), October 3, 2010 (Roger Snodgrass), January 27, 2011 (Ana Marie Trujillo), January 30, 2011 (Ana Marie Trujillo)

Petitition Against Discontinuing Post Office at Los Pinos, Rio Arriba, 1931. Governor Arthur Seligman Papers. New Mexico State Records Center and Archives.

Map: Rand McNally & Co. New Mexico, 1879

CPSIA information can be obtained at www.ICGtesting.com
Printed in the USA
LVOW041445270912

300607LV00011B/8/P